THE MANY
LAYERED
SKIRT

THE MANY
LAYERED
SKIRT

DÀN GĀO QÚN

MARLENE F CHENG

To order additional copies of this book, contact:
Xlibris Corporation
1-888-795-4274
www.Xlibris.com
Orders@Xlibris.com
112909

CONTENTS

Dedication

In Memory of My Brother
Man Kit Cheng
June 30th, 1923-December 8th, 1945.

(Kit in his Chinese National Air Force uniform)

Kit lives as a memory to inspire us all to find our own
passion and to become the best we can be in life.

"Flight is freedom in its purest form,
To dance with the clouds which follow a storm;
To roll and glide, to wheel and spin,
To feel the joy that swells within;
To leave the earth with its troubles and fly,
And know the warmth of a clear spring sky;
Then back to earth at the end of a day,
Released from the tensions which melted away.
Should my end come while I am in flight,
Whether brightest day or darkest night;
Spare me your pity and shrug off the pain,
Secure in the knowledge that I'd do it again;
For each of us is created to die,
And within me I know,
I was born to fly."

Impression of a pilot (untitled)
(author unknown)

INTRODUCTION

I had heard "bits and pieces" of Kwan stories ever since I met Ching (Richmond) in 1957. Then with the influx of family friends and relatives from Hong Kong to Vancouver in the 1960s more of "this and that" got added. However, when the siblings gathered, and inevitably would reminisce, I would make myself scarce, as I knew their memories were best caressed by their native tongue, and I didn't speak Cantonese. However, when their mother came to live with us, she told me many stories while we wrapped won ton, or when she was ironing Ching's underwear, which I adamantly refused to do. She had had servants all her life, and held high standards of housekeeping. When she came to Canada, she divided the remaining "red and black" dishes and gave a set to each of her sons, so I heard the dish's story at that time. She was the one who told me about Honkie's original Emily Carr painting. I have no idea what became of it; however, I do know what became of the Blue Boy and Matching Girl pictures that hung in Grandauntie # 10's room. Their mother gave them to me when she was allocating her worldly things. I took the liberty and included the dishes, the painting and the pictures in Man Sheung's writings. I felt that they were an integral part and shouldn't be left out.

Nonetheless, all of these tidbits of information that I had gleaned over the years, didn't prepare me, in any way, to face the challenge that Man Sheung presented me with. The Kwan family was having a reunion, and she had been asked to write some of her memories. She said that she had a few stray thoughts—snippets of memory. These stray snippets came in a mountainous pile of hand-written foolscap pages that had been cut and pasted so many times that no two pages were the same shape or size, and the pages hadn't been numbered. Man Sheung is an artist, and she definitely has an "artsy mind". Her thinking is flowery, and her thoughts jump "helter-skelter," and her writing follows; wherever, her thoughts wander. These wanderings took place from the Qin Dynasty to the present day, but were concentrated (thank goodness) on the few years before, through to a few years after, the Japanese invasion of China. Man Sheung's challenge—she wanted me to take her information, and to put it into story form, in time for the reunion.

My first task was to find some chronological order. After many attempts and after giving up many times, I decided I should just throw the pages down the stairs, and start writing from the bottom step up. However, I persevered, and using a large pin board and yards of coloured strings, I eventually decided when things; probably, happened. I tell you all this as a way of explaining, that I own any errors that occur.

You have to understand that Man Sheung lives in Singapore, and I was editing in Canada, and that we are both computer illiterate, and a phone call meant that it was the middle of the night for one of us.

I got involved. The happenings became interesting. I began to feel that I knew the people—some of them intimately. I was astonished how Man Sheung could find small pleasures in a world that had gone mad. Perhaps it was her saving grace. Her sharing of these bits of happiness was a welcome intrusion into the horrific happenings and the almost, at times, unbearable sadness. Then I became obsessed—I wanted Man Sheung's snippets to be an honest rendering of her thoughts and feelings, as she remembered them. This is not a Kwan Genealogy Record. This is Man Sheung's story. And she hopes that it fills your expectations, and she wishes you all a Happy Reunion.

Marlene Cheng
Vancouver, B.C.
July 25, 2011

DÀN GĀO QÚN

The Many Layered Skirt

I sat, holding the scissors, awaiting the next cutting assignment, shifting ever more precariously to the edge of the three-legged stool, borrowed from the kitchen, as Grandauntie # 10, seeming tireless, spoke non-stop, needing to get it all said, as if her train of thought, once interrupted, would need more fuel than she was capable of mustering, to get it started again. She did her sewing in the same manner—I would, most often, need to start the treadle, but once she got going, she was off to the races, and I might need to help her stop, to twist the material around, and to turn the wheel for a few back stitches—to secure her efforts.

When my mother arrived here at # 115 Waterloo Road, Kowloon Tong with six kids in tow, she took over the household duties, freeing up Grandauntie # 10 to concentrate on her church and charity work. At the moment, Grandauntie # 10 was sewing patchwork items and baptismal gowns for the missionary group—the "Little Flock." I deliver these, along with some food items, by bicycle, around the Garden Triangle, down the tree-lined Cumberland Road, past Boundary, to the church. Over the few years that I have been doing this, I have come to know the missionaries very well. If it is hot, they treat me to cold lemonade. If cold, something hot, and we chat awhile. When I explained to them that I would be coming less and less, they understood—they knew that Grandauntie # 10 had Parkinson's, and that her health problems were progressing. I was to have an adventitious, lucky, most unexpected meeting with the "Little Flock," far off from this place, in the interior of mainland China, during the war . . . but I mustn't get ahead of myself.

I sat on the stool. Grandauntie # 10 spoke. She had urgency about her. She needed to tell me about her family, as if her mother and father would be forgotten—not paid their just dues—if she didn't pass on everything she remembered about them, and she mustn't dally. She was most anxious to talk about her mother, maybe because she held her in such high regard (not that she didn't her father, but being a woman and so ahead of her time, her mother must be remembered, if only as an example—she was proof in the pudding that Chinese women could be influential, even in a male dominated culture). If Grandauntie # 10 only had time left to tell one of their stories, it was going to be her mother's, my Great Grandmother's (Kwan Amui Lai, 1840-1902):

If I was going to understand my Great Grandmother's story, I had to know what was happening in China at the time when she was a young girl. "Besides," Grandauntie # 10 said, "A little history lesson can't be a bad thing." She told me that during the mid-1800s, foreign countries were trying to take over the coastal regions, and were trading opium to China. This resulted in the Opium War (1841) and the six "Unfair Concessions or Treaties." Paralleling these happenings, a scholar wrote an essay, and passed it around to the literate of the Peking Imperial Examination Hall. This essay questioned the old tradition of "Totalitarian Rule", and discussed Democracy and Christianity as the awakening of "new" thinking for the people of China. It so happened, that at this time, a Mr. Hong was at the Imperial Hall, and was much impressed by this essay, and formed his own Christian Army called "Heavenly Peace." The ideology of this movement was human rights and Mr. Hong's version of Christianity. This group, wearing their signature yellow scarves, met the British boats that were carrying opium, and burned, on the beaches, the opium and the British flag. Recruiting, converting and frightening, they rampaged through remote villages. Society, in general, was very confused over all this "new" thinking. Many thought it was the foreigner's way of trying to take over their country, and labeled groups like the "Yellow Scarves" the "Foreign Devils."

Because of the rampaging Christian armies, Great Grandmother Kwan's father decided to take his wife and two small children to the city of Canton, to seek some law and order. Somehow, on the journey, the father and daughter got separated from the mother and son. Being hungry and tired, the daughter sat down on some doorsteps. The lady of the house promised to mind the little girl, while the father retraced his steps, looking for the others. This lady was Mrs. Cotswold. Her husband was in charge of the British Affairs in the Colony of Hong Kong, and they were in Canton learning Cantonese. The father never returned for his daughter;

thus, Great Grandmother Kwan was raised by the Cotswolds, who later returned to Hong Kong. Tutors were brought to their house, so she could be well educated after the British fashion: she was given piano lessons; became fluent in French and English as well as in her native Cantonese. This privileged, little, Chinese girl, was well steeped in English tea and in Christian values, as the Cotswolds were staunch Christians.

Not much sewing got done at this session, but Grandauntie # 10 seemed pleased that she had finally started to tell me about her mother, and now it was time for dinner. Even though, we did the sewing downstairs on the dining-room table, there was no need to pack away our things. The dining room, like the living room, carpeted wall to wall, elegantly furnished in contemporary London style, was seldom used—we took our meals upstairs with Ah Dong. When I first came to this house, at the age of five (1930), after leaving my father's house in Kuala Lumpur, and travelling, on a large white ocean liner, with three blue chimneys, to Hong Kong, I was very impressed—this house was big, elegant and spacious.

The house I left in Kuala Lumpur, by comparison, was over-crowded with practicality. In this house, there was a most fascinating grandfather clock that sat on the floor, and stood four feet tall; there were shelves for silver and crystal; there was a writing desk, and displayed on it was a picture of a beautiful young lady. On the way up the stairs, to dinner, I noticed the other clock, much smaller than the grandfather. It had cute birds that came out to announce the time—at least it did have, before my brother Kit and his Muslim friend, Ah Soh, took it apart, in their secret place, up in the attic, and didn't get it back together quite right. For that project, gone awry, Kit earned a seat in the time-out-thinking-chair. He was like a joyful jack-in-the-box, popping in and out of that chair, on a regular basis. It wasn't a hard-backed-sit-up-straight kind of chair or a dunce's stool, but was an over-stuffed, green, comfy, big-old-one, and I would see him in it, looking like a contortionist, his long limbs hanging askew, every which way, or he would be standing on his head, his legs curled tight up to his chest; as if, he was flying upside down in his imaginary airplane, that he always talked about. I felt sorry for him. I needn't have. He said that in the chair, he had time to plan his next project. Ideas came to him non-stop; as if, he had a hot line to the universe, and he was always tapped in. As luck would have it, he had his friend Ah Soh—his cat's paw. Kit was the go-to-man for ideas, you went to Ah Soh if you needed to get something done—completed.

The eating place upstairs was small and intimate; nonetheless, Ah Dong insisted that we be taught proper table manners: adults first; proper handling of the chopsticks; please and thank you; decorum and dignity. He was particular about his table. He liked simple dishes, meticulously prepared, and we children, starving and anxious to dig in, would have to sit patiently and wait, if the dish was ill-prepared, for the server to take it back down the stairs, along the outside corridor, next to the maids quarters, to the kitchen, at the back of the house, so that the two cooks could fix it, and then, having to retrace his steps could again present the dish for Ah Dong's approval—it's a wonder we had any dishes hot.

You might wonder who this Ah Dong is, and why we were living in his house. He is my mother's uncle, her father's brother, my Granduncle # 13. Ah Dong is a name of endearment—we all love him, but because he is very strict, we children also call him "The Dictator." After the birth of her seventh child, my mother's mother died, and so, mother and her younger sister Violet, were raised in this house (# 115 Waterloo Road) by Grandaunt and Granduncle # 13 (Ah Dong), who had only one child of their own, a son, my Uncle Honkie, who spent his younger years in boarding school, in London, and only came home on an occasional holiday.

And why were we living in Ah Dong's house? Mother and father had agreed that we children must have a formal Chinese education.

For this, we needed to leave Kuala Lumpur and father, and come to Hong Kong. Mother would naturally bring us here to # 115 to the "parents" that raised her. She arrived with Kit (8), Mungie (2), me (5) and three nieces—her brother Kin-Tong's children. We were greeted by Grandauntie #10, and she gave me, instead of the usual red packet, three monkey statues. You know the ones, see-no-evil, hear-no-evil and speak-no-evil. At the age of five, I didn't understand the significance of these statues. I was more interested in running around this spacious house; finding secret nooks and crannies for hide-and-seek; sitting beside the grandfather clock waiting for the birds to come out; playing out in the huge yard, with the swing, see-saw, sandpit and clay pot, big enough for Kit to sail his toy boats and; of course, I loved going across Waterloo Road, up the hill, to Mary Hill Convent to school with the nuns. But now, at the age of eleven, I appreciate Ah Dong's yard for other things: its neatly trimmed bamboo hedge, so impressive from the road; its manicured lawn, surrounded by two rows of coloured grasses; its fruit trees and beautiful flowering shrubs. I can sit up where the branches fork, in my favorite tree—the peach, and eat, au naturel, the fruit, fuzz and all, juices running down my arms, that I can lick clean, as far as my tongue can reach. Or, I can escape to the wisteria-covered, wrap-around front-porch, lovely in the afternoon, with sunlight finding ways passed the branches and clusters of violet-blue flowers to form ever shifting patterns across the floor and up the wall, as the day progresses. I can curl up in strategic spots, and daydream my favorite story—the shadow play of the beautiful, young, Chinese girl, who to spare her aging father, cuts off her hair and goes to war. Depending on the wind and the movement of the patterns, she accomplishes many brave feats and returns home to accolades galore—knighted on the shoulder with her sword. She is my heroine. The porch was lovely these afternoons, touched with the mystery and magic that lies at the center of all loveliness.

But there isn't much down time, "The Dictator," with his traditional Chinese thinking well mixed with his Christian beliefs, is determined to guide, gently but strictly, our education. He leaves nothing to chance—he disciplines us. Every morning we grind our ink, and practice calligraphy; twice a week a master is brought in to drill us in Classical Chinese Concepts. Kit will sit under the cloth-covered table to whisper answers to me, while the master parades around the room with his "stick" at ready to bang me on the head, when I answer incorrectly. Kit says, "If I don't help her, she'll get a hole in the head from all the banging," and every week day; of course, we go to Pui Ching Middle School, not across the street anymore, but by bus, some distance away, past Boundary, at the far end of Waterloo Road.

I said before, that at five, I didn't understand the significance of the three monkey statues, but now, I think I know what Grandauntie #10 was trying to explain to me.

I've come to know the other Kwans that live on Waterloo Road—in total, at any one time, about fifteen uncles and aunts (some plain and some grand) and a swarm of young ones, and we move quite freely from one household to the other. She didn't want me tittle-tattling—carrying gossip from one house to the next, speaking ill of anyone, not seeing the best qualities in people, expressing strong opinions—best to listen and learn. She felt that see-no-evil, hear-no-evil, speak-no-evil expressed exactly what she was trying to say. As a reminder, I keep the monkeys, on the dressing table, in the downstairs bedroom, that I share with other girl cousins—Cheuk and Chit and sometimes Eleanor, from the Cheng side of the family. We love the four-poster brass beds—from London, we assume.

When I finally got the chance to help Grandauntie # 10 with her sewing again, I was surprised when she started talking about her father. I thought she had only just begun with her mother, but, for whatever reason, she alone knows, she started with, "Today, I will tell you about my father, Kwan Yuen-Cheong, 1832-1912." I put down the scissors; slipped from the stool; made myself comfortable on the wall-to-wall carpet. Sunlight was bouncing off a beautifully cut crystal vase, on the shelf, and I painted, in my mind's eye, with all the colours of the rainbow, the history lesson that she always began her stories with:

The London Missionaries had been in China for some time, and had converted ten Chinese to Christianity. I gave the missionaries cerulean habits, and where there should have been white, I painted bright yellow. My Grandfather—Kwan Yat, 1797-1863 was one of these ten, and was the first Christian in the Kwan Family. I painted the ten in red traditional cheongsams, and gave Kwan a big golden "1" to hang around his neck like a cross. The "1's" son, my father, was doubtful of his father's new faith. He could see what the foreign invasions were doing to his country. He could see the confusion in the thinking of the people. I had great fun imagining him—I painted him chartreuse with darker green Doubting Thomas figures (Janus heads looking both ways) on his skirts and on his chaplet. He too wondered if it was all a "foreign devil" plot to take over China. These "foreign devils," weird white creatures with wings, leapt and flew about the room in red and black plaid monkey suits, their tails swinging 'round and 'round. And, where was it written?—this new salvation. Then, my father became aware of one Benjamin Morrison, who on a handmade printing press, in a small room of a Christian school, in Hong Kong, was translating the Bible from English into Chinese. I gave Benjamin Morrison, western clothes of indigo and placed a golden trident (the trilogy) in his hand and a violet halo 'round his head. My father went to help Benjamin Morrison. It was twenty-five years in the translation, but finally in 1867 the first Chinese Bible was published, and father, in the process, had become a devout Christian.

Being so busy in my imagination, I only got the jist of Grandauntie # 10's story, but, in any case, her finishing point was probably, the most important. She told me that the privileged, little, Chinese girl, who was so well steeped in English tea and Christian values, having been raised by the Cotwolds, married her father who was also a Christian, but was mostly dipped in traditional, classical, Chinese ways.

Noting that I hadn't cut even one piece of cloth, and she hadn't sewed even two together, we decided to call it a day. I could bring her tea, upstairs in her room; she would rest, as Honkie was coming home soon, and she needed to conserve her energy. If I didn't mind, maybe I could help her with the stairs. I wondered how many more sewing sessions there would be—I must pay more attention.

I've told you that, over time, I came to know the other Kwans on Waterloo road. We went often to # 101—Grandpa Kwan's, the house that mother and Auntie Violet left, as young girls, when they went to live at # 115. Grandpa Kwan is loving and kind and gentle. When we were little, we thought him quite comical, with his snow white hair and his arm going up and down, so that his fingers could curl his equally white mustache, when he smiled. I was the Queen of England, when I had the rare chance to ride in his big, black, shiny car, with a flag on it and a white-uniformed chauffeur at the wheel. I would do the "Royal Wave," and Oh! How I wanted a fancy big hat, with a beautiful silk flower—one side of the hat turned up, the other side turned down.

Now, I drop by Grandpa's house at will. When I'm returning, after my delivery to the "Little Flock," all hot from bicycling up hill, I often stop by. Today, I found Grandma Kwan in her garden: she had a red hibiscus flower tucked in her hair, just above the ear. I told her how lovely she looked—just like a Hawaiian lady. She had cold lemonade brought, and we sat on the garden bench, near the lei-scent of the plumeria. She had been picking hibiscus and calendula; she would soak the petals, and then, after being out in the sun, she washed her face and any exposed areas with it. She carried with her the folklore of nature that had been passed down through the women of her family. I was fascinated by her stories and by her potions, creams and tisanes. She would never let me take notes—to remember is to know, she would remind me. I watched her many times as she squeezed the juice from the aloe succulent and mixed it with the juices from pestled mint leaves and stirred the concoction into a base to make a hydrating cream, and like-wise she mixed green tea and ginger. She would break a piece from the aloe, and rub it on a bee sting for instant relief. I never saw her make tisanes, as they were made fresh when someone had an ailment. I do know that she made one from the passion flower for Grandauntie #10's Parkinson's Disease—it was suppose to have anti-spasmodic qualities. I don't know if Grandauntie #10 took it to please Grandma Kwan, or because the passion flower represented a token of Christ's passion—that is, his redemption of unenlightened humanity through the gift of his supreme suffering and sacrifice.

Grandma Kwan explained how the different parts of the flower represented Christ: The leaf—the spear that pierced Christ's side: The five anthers—the five wounds; The tendrils—whips: The stamens—hammers; The three styles—three nails; The fleshy threads within the flowers—crown of thorns; The calyx—glory; The white tint—purity; The blue tint—heaven; The strange and delightful perfume—the incense of earthly atoms transmuting to spiritual atoms in the resurrection. Grandauntie # 10 was impressed, and she drank the tisane with delight. As we sipped our lemonade, Grandma was telling me why there were a few lemons left up high on the tree. I thought that they had been out of reach. "You never take all the fruit from a tree," she explained. "You must leave some for the tree fairies, and then, you will be assured of a good crop next year." She was showing me how to squint my eyes to see the energy moving in and out from the trees, when, from out of no where, she said, "You know, "I *am*—Hawaiian." "Oh?" "Please tell me." And so, thrilled with the rapture of it all—the garden, the scent and her intriguing wisdom, I sipped my cold drink; listened, and Grandma Kwan spoke:

She told me that her ancestors were from the three rivers area of China. They were boat people or Kat. Like gypsies, they lived on their houseboats, and sailed to wherever work could be found, feeding themselves from the water, fresh fish and water-weed. "Somehow," she said. "My relatives sailed far, and ended up in Hawaii." She was lost in thought for awhile, and I was busy picturing these families, on their small boats, crossing all that way. "And," she finally went on. "Your Grandpa's first wife was also from Hawaii." She really had my interest now. "That means, you also have Hawaiian blood." "Tell me!" "Tell me!" Instead, she told me that to get the facts straight, I should ask Grandpa, or even mother, surely they knew the story better than she. I had to push my bicycle home: I would have fallen off: I was in cloud cuckoo land, with all the fantasies swirling around in my head.

With the pretence of checking to see if her thermos needed to be filled; immediately, having arrived home, I went up to Grandauntie # 10's room. She was at the desk reading her Bible. Not minding the intrusion, she set about to talking. I, wasting no opportunity, pounced. "Tell me about Grandpa Kwan, about his marriages." But first, to keep everything in sequence, lest she forget, she wanted to tell me about her own parent's marriage. "And, about your Grandfather's," she said. "Be patient, I'll surely get to that, time allowing."

She told me, that when her mother and father were first married (1867), they lived on 1st Street in Hong Kong, on the ground floor of an apartment building; that her mother worked as a nurse at Nethersole Hospital, and later became the hospital matron.

I should go look at the early hospital records. There is an insert that reads something like: "There was in the hospital, in the woman's ward, a Matron, a Mrs. Kwan, a Chinese lady of wonderful intelligence and ability, born hundreds of years before her time."

She continued: In time, they had fifteen children, and were forced to move to the top floor. We called it the "attic"—a bigger space which was still affordable because of the inconvenience of many stairs. At that time, Hong Kong had a water distribution problem. There was one public faucet per street, and the residents had to line up for water, and had to carry it home. All those stairs! Mother taught us team work and cooperation: we made an assembly line up the stairs—problem solved. She used the same practical problem solving when it came to our education. She formed us into teams; one member of each team went to school; came home and taught the other members of his team the day's lessons. The next year a different member went to school. In this manner all fifteen of us (including the girls who weren't allowed to go to school) got twelve years of Classical Chinese Education. This pleased father, because, even though he was a Christian, he believed that Christianity and westernized thinking would undermine the traditional social system, and so was adamant that we have a firm foundation in the old culture. Mother, probably because of her British upbringing, felt that if we were to manage in the changing world, we needed more. She was successful in teaching # 1, # 5, and # 15 both French and English. She convinced father to send # 6 to Northern China to school. He was one of the first graduates from the Imperial Medical School at Tientsin, and became the personal physician to the Empress Dowager. Later, # 12, # 13, # 14 and # 15 followed in # 6's footsteps and went to Tientsin to school. She stopped abruptly and said, "It must be time for dinner." "But Grandauntie # 10," I protested. "You didn't even mention # 7, Grandpa Kwan, let alone tell me about his marriages." "Because, you see, he was at the British (Alice) Medical School, and hadn't met his wife yet. In good time. In good time."

Bringing his Degree in Architecture from Cambridge and his beautiful, young, British bride, Uncle Honkie; finally, came home. In anticipation of this homecoming, the house had been all a flutter. The upstairs-back-bedroom had been emptied of its storage, scrubbed to the nines, newly curtained and bedspreaded. Our personal maids (Little Snow and Lucky One) didn't know quite what a young British lady might like, but Ah Dong, who had studied at the London School of Economics, and feeling himself fluent in English ways, guided them. They did their best. In hopes of ridding the room of its Lysol smell, before the guests arrived, I went every day to open the windows, stretching across the wall, overlooking the back garden, to let in fresh air and the scent from the rhododendron that was in full bloom below. Uncle Honkie and Margeta nested well in this bride's chamber, and let the house flutter as it would. Being a not-quite-yet teenager, I was mesmerized by Margeta.

Her hair was blond like honey, when you pour it from the storage crock, with the metal clasps, against the ants, into the morning bowl, on the tray, that I took up to her, on Ah Dong's suggestion, thinking that she might find Oriental breakfast strange. There was also, white-bread toast, English tea, milk and sugar. She let her hair that waved naturally down to its tips, flow as it might—unbridled, especially at breakfast. Her skin was the rhododendron blossom—a delicate white-pink—flawless. Her blue, blue (azure like the sky) eyes twinkled that first morning, charming and friendly, as we passed the tray back and forth, using the only common words we could muster in our shyness—Thank you. Thank you. But right from the start, we became close friends, and took breakfast together in their room, windows wide opened, and we left the congie to the others.

Ah Dong hosted a big family gathering at his favorite restaurant (Summer Palace) in honour of the wedding and the homecoming of the bride and groom. Uncle Honkie was something like the prodigal son—come home. He had been in England for such a long time: had grown independent of the family. The grown-ups took up two, large, round tables; the young ones pushed two smaller ones close so that we could all chat together. Manners didn't suddenly fly out the window, but without the "adults first" rule, we, laughing and joyfully teasing each other unchecked, ate in earnest, and our dishes emptied far more quickly than the adult's.

Ah Dong explained to Margeta the significance of each dish. With varying degrees of fluency, most everyone 'round the table spoke English, but they slipped easily back into the familiarity of their native tongue, and

Honkie was left to attend Margeta. He gave her small portions, and if need be, she could pass unwanted food back to his bowl, discreetly. She politely declined the black, slippery, Chinese mushrooms and the similarly looking abalone. Well in advance of the dinner, she had explained to Honkie that she couldn't possibly eat anything that had been regurgitated by a bird, so Ah Dong had pre-ordered winter melon soup. The proud melon, serrated 'round its top, stood a foot tall, and was filled with a delicate soup afloat with tiny dices of lotus seeds, grass mushrooms, abalone, bamboo shoots, ginger, duck and chicken breasts, Chinese ham and spring onions. The presentation was so grand, and the soup, with melon scrapings, so delicious, that no one missed the famous Bird's Nest. Margeta couldn't swallow the hundred-year-old-egg delicacy, and she quickly slipped it into her table napkin, draped coyly over her mouth, and wondered what was wrong with the fresh eggs of Hong Kong. She knew that there were local hen houses, and that chickens ran free-range in many backyards—why would they have to preserve eggs for a hundred years? She; politely, didn't ask. At the end of the dinner, she ate the long noodles to assure a long and happy marriage, and we all went back to Grandpa Kwan's house for chrysanthemum tea; or, if caffeine was a problem, for freshly-ground, ice-cold soya-milk, and to smell Grandma Kwan's fully in bloom and highly scented Night Jessamine, and mother had promised to recite a poem.

Her English was impeccable. Ah Dong had had his two girls tutored. They learnt English by memorizing and reciting poetry.

We huddled in to every available space in the living—and dining-rooms, some of us even on the floor, cross-legged lotus-style, and took our drinks. Then, it was time to trek out to the garden. Uncle # 16, still in his Boy Scout uniform and with a torch; excitedly, tried to herd us along the paving stones. Our eyes, trying to adjust to the dark, reached the simmering-white moon garden, centered by the Night Jessamine, fan-trellised to the back wall, footed by other white flowers—angels'-trumpets, gardenia, special white-variegated-leaf hosta, jasmine and sweet-scented phlox, first. By the time our bodies had caught up, we had waddled along in blindness, half-on-half-off the stones, like the Mandarin ducks I once saw, up the hill, at the dairy farm. When we reached this white garden, we dipped our noses to take in the scent, not unlike the ducks dipping their beaks at the feeding trough. When we had dipped, we moved further along the stones to allow those that came behind their turn at dipping. When we couldn't possibly exclaim any longer over the Night Jessamine's attributes, especially her scent, which we had lifted as high as the heavens, we pondered over which poem mother might recite, and then turned, reversed our duck-waddle back to the house, anxious to find a space near where mother would perform. Uncle # 16, who had boisterously voted for Kipling's "If," surprised us. We had no idea that he had a word of English, but apparently he was studying this poem in his English class, and he was unusually attentive. Being the youngest of sixteen children, he was always called "The Baby," which he detested; so, Kipling's last line appealed to him: "And so, you'll be a man, my son."—he so much wanted to become Kipling's "man." When he reached the house he had grass-cuttings-bedraggled, dew-sodden, best-shoes that a servant quickly rescued to be dried and re-polished for his next school day.

Mother started with Longfellow's:

> Listen my children and you shall hear
> Of the midnight ride of Paul Revere; . . .

The adults were taken by surprise: they thought that mother only knew English poets. The young people loved it; especially, the young men and boys who heard:

> . . . the hurrying hoof-beats of that steed . . .

onomatopoeically throughout the recitation, and probably, imagined themselves upon that horse, waving their swords, heroically saving the world.

Not Kit, of course, he was a high-flier, no horse for him—he would fly, but not on top of something that had hoofs on the ground. When mother had finished, her father said, "Well done Dai Day. I hope you aren't foreshadowing a Chinese hero, who might come riding by,

> 'A knock at the door, and a word that shall echo for evermore,'

warning us of a Japanese invasion." Mother laughed off the gloominess of her father's words, and went on in a more cheery note, and to suit the English buffs, with Wordsworth's:

I wandered lonely as a cloud
That floats on high o'er vales and hills,
When all at once I saw a crowd,
A host, of golden daffodils; . . .
And then my heart with pleasure fills,
and dances with the daffodils.

Her father was again pleased; it was obvious that they shared a special bond. She had a strong interest in medicine, and they could talk endlessly about disease and cures. Sitting next to Grandpa Kwan was Wai, his pharmacist, who was always included, as family, at these gatherings. He had been with Grandpa Kwan as long as any one could remember. He and Grandpa Kwan shared a steadfast loyalty—I was curious about that too.

Then the party settled into its usual after dinner talk. The siblings were very fond of each other, and enjoyed reminiscing about their childhood and growing up days. "Tell everyone, #13, how you got into that British school, and paved the way for # 12 and me," started Grandpa Kwan. "Except for the little that passed our resistance at home, from mother and # 5's hasty-last-minute tutoring attempts, we got most of our English at that school," he added. # 13 looked at his watch, and hesitated, but everyone knew, that Grandpa Kwan had set the bait, and #13 was hooked. "We all had twelve years of Chinese school already," he started. "But you know mother, she was one determined lady. Because I was the shortest and had a baby face, she decided, that I should be the one to try to gain entrance. She took me to the second-hand bookstore on Boundary, at the bottom of Katorie Hill where the school was; bought books for all the classes. # 5 got me started with the English ones, and then I would go up to D.H.O. (Diocesan Home and Orphanage), and sit outside under the windows, and listen. Remember how there was that covered-by-the-roof-wrap-around-balcony and those huge, curved-at-the-top, deep-set windows—did they have glass? They were always open." "You're the engineer," spoke up # 12. "We are mere physicians. How would we know?"

Everyone had a chuckle, and more tea was poured. "Anyway," continued # 13. "I sat the entrance examinations, and everything after that is history. You two got accepted on my strong back. Sun was there at the same time, probably in '83." We knew that he was referring to Dr. Sun Yat Sen, and Cheuk and I exchanged glances. "Yes," said Grandpa Kwan. "But, his

English was much better than ours. Ever since he came back from Hawaii, # 5 tutored him. He worshipped mother, you know. He was always telling me how he admired her understanding of western and eastern cultures and her advanced forward thinking. She must have influenced him with her charity and steadfast faith as well. He became a Christian, and even asked her to be his godmother. He pointed out to me what is written in the historical Hong Kong Blue Book about her. Apparently, she was an interpreter and a go-between in the court during the land disputes between the foreign invaders and the Chinese." "I know," interrupted # 13. "I had it copied, it reads something like:

> 'Imagine, especially in those times, this petite intelligent lady
> with an understanding of both cultures standing up in court
> to interpret the issues. She fearlessly attempted to bridge the
> inevitable cultural differences with true justice'."

"And," went on Grandpa Kwan, "I think that mother's early influence and all the western political ideas he picked up at D.H.O. and at Alice, fueled his eventual revolutionary endeavours. He was very clever. He talked politics constantly, would chew your ear off all night, and write medical examinations the next day, and be top in the class. I was indebted to him—he introduced me to my first wife—your grandmother—girls." He was addressing Cheuk and me. I went straight up, in one fell swoop, from lotus position to arms and hands above the head, tippy-toed on the diving board, and if I had gone off, it wouldn't have been an elegant dive, but a great insensible swoon to land in the water, like a jelly fish. Here it comes, I thought, my Hawaiian blood gurgling; if indeed, I had any. And, right from the horse's mouth. "Sun was always drumming up money for his revolutionary cause," Grandpa Kwan said. "And a well established plantation owner in Hawaii donated generously, and he came to Hong Kong to check up on Sun, and brought his two daughters with him." Grandpa Kwan, curling his neat and already securely in place mustache, took a drink of tea. I, gasping for breath, so as not to drown, and as inconspicuously as the situation could possibly afford, fell down upon Cheuk. Grandpa Kwan started up again, "It wasn't your typical arranged marriage: I had met the daughters when Sun introduced me to the father. They were striking beauties, and after Sun plied me with their attributes, I couldn't resist when he asked if I might marry the one that wanted to stay behind in Hong Kong, when the father returned home. That's how I met and married your grandmother—she was part Chinese, part Caucasian and part Hawaiian. She was pregnant with you Dai Day, when I moved my practice to Chang Wong, very near Nan King, to help Sun, when he became Provisional President of The First Republic.

Those were heady days. I had a wonderful wife and family, and I paid my debt to Sun. But, those stories are for another night. It's getting late, and # 13 is nodding off." "I'm not nodding off," twisted back # 13. "I know all those stories, I was just waiting to tell you about my termite problem, and now you are shooing us home." "What's your problem?" asked # 12 sympathetically. "I have termites in the soil in the back garden, and they are eating the timber part of the kitchen." "If you would stop Ah Soh from chasing away the birds, the birds would eat the termites." Grandpa Kwan jumped in, and then using very cleverly chosen play-on-words in Chinese, he offered: "Take your pick, birds on the wing and no "holy" fruit or wingless birds and no flying ants." It loses, probably everything in the translation, but everyone got the jist, and being well satiated, we said our goodnights.

Cheuk and I fell into our lovely brass bed, with me up against the wall. After having drunk so much tea, I probably would have to climb over her many times in the night. But, as it turned out, we whispered back and forth till morning, so getting up to the toilet wasn't an issue. We loved our Hawaiian blood; we loved our big Kwan family; we marveled at the opportunities that they had all been given, and how they seized the day and were so successful; we decided that if it weren't for our Great Grandparents things would have been different—they broke the traditional Chinese family mould. We both knew that Great Grandfather, after he was married, returned to school, and became a dentist in order to support the fifteen children and to serve his community. He came to the realization that education and service and Christianity were important, so he had the Kwan Family Motto changed from "Nation and School" to "Stay Firm in Christian Faith and Contribute to Nation and Society." We agreed that everyone, after the great grandparents and before us, had done the motto proud, and now it was up to our generation. We vowed to each other to work hard at school, and definitely, we must improve our English. The next time we went to Grandpa Kwan to ask for extra pocket money to go to a movie Hong Kong side, we would ask him in English. We giggled a little, as girls will do, and we imagined all sorts of things about Uncle Honkie and his bride, and then it was morning, and we fell asleep.

As a wedding present, mother had promised the newly weds some dishes. These weren't just any dishes—they were special. I was still sleeping, and missed the conversation about the dishes, but Margeta, being very excited over them, was only to happy to share the story: Apparently, mother's # 6 Uncle (the one that had been the physician to the Empress Dowager) had given mother many, many, many place settings as her wedding present. Every year, the Empress Dowager had a new, double-set of dishes made for the palace, and because she was pleased with her personal physician, she gave him a set. The number of pieces was uncountable. Mother's arrived from Peking with the Imperial stamp on the many crates.

Skipping the tedious job of checking each crate for its contents, she had, at random, chosen some to be sent to her new home in Kuala Lumpur, and the rest she left in a go-down. In Kuala Lumpur, she had many bowls, twelve soup tureens, a number of spoons and little else, so she always used these dishes for soup at the beginning of a dinner, and switched to other patterns as the meal progressed. It was to become the highly fashionable thing to do. And tureens filled with floating flowers were mother's signature conversation piece. She wanted Honkie and Margeta to go through the crates with her, and to choose what they wanted: she knew there were some cups, with handles in the English style, and saucers to match, that they might like. To Honkie's architectural eye, the crates themselves had great appeal. He was designing a home for Margeta, and was always looking at things from that perspective. He and mother had a very easy relationship: they were obviously fond of each other. He, mischievously and with his adopted British humour, referred to the dishes as the "Queen's Plate" and mother, not sure if he was referring to Victoria or to the Dowager, always replied, that he had been in the London fog too long. When they brought home their choices, I recognized the pattern: I remembered it from Kuala Lumpur. On a shiny licorice-black background there was painted a profusion of various coloured flowers. Peonies, the prominent ones, were quite large, and were dark reddish-pink, fading to a lighter shade. I hadn't noticed before, but, when I held a dainty pouring pot, I could feel that the flowers were raised—many layers of porcelain paint had been applied, I assumed. I also noticed that each piece was slightly different. They must have been individually painted. The pouring pot had a lid with a T-shaped petit knob for lifting, and it had a tiny flower painted across it. I would like to be able to paint on porcelain, I thought. I would do a whole set, and without any warning, hot tears formed behind my eyes, and a profound sadness washed over me. I ran quickly from the house, and escaped to the most secret place on the porch, under the wisteria. The tears flowed, and I convulsed with great gasping sobs. I wasn't here to escape into fantasy. I had to face reality. I had to find a way to deal with it. I've been avoiding telling what happened, but cocooned in the wisteria, having spent all the tears, that I didn't even realize I hadn't shed, I think I can now talk about it. It was 1937, and father thought that the Japanese might invade Hong Kong, so he brought us back to Kuala Lumpur. Cousin Eleanor's mother had recently been killed in a car accident, so feeling responsible for Eleanor, and thinking because she was a young girl she would be vulnerable, mother cut off Eleanor's long hair; gave her Mungie's passport, and took her with us, and left Mungie behind, to be with Ah Dong. Father arranged English tutors for us—the first formal instructions that I had in English. We were re-acquainted with the Yap family next door. Auntie Emily (the mother) and her twin sister and mother were like sisters—the triplets. Paul, Raymond and Phoebe (the children) treated Ching (my youngest brother-sometimes referred to as Richmond) like a younger brother.

Ching would walk across the narrow veranda ledges from one house to the other; as if, both houses were his. The older kids ran along underneath to catch him, if he should fall. Mother was again able to use the black and red dishes.

But all this didn't last long. Father decided that the Japanese were concentrating on the mainland, and that it was safe for us to return to Hong Kong. On our way back, we met father in Macau—his birth place. Father was proud to show us the big mansion, which was his boyhood home, and point out the street that was named after his grandfather. He wanted to take us to the ancient family village, but we had to settle for a view of it from high ground in Macau. That's when mother told us, that father had graduated from Illinois State University in Chicago: he was in the banking business in Kuala Lumpur: he had many property holdings and shares in tin mining—he was influential. And because there had been many kidnappings, it was unsafe for him to go to the village. We were in Macau not much more then a month and I remember the lovely Colonial-Portuguese house where we stayed. It was there that I learnt the little I know of the Cheng family history. Father had three siblings (one sister was Eleanor's mother). Their mother died during the smallpox epidemic, and they were raised by their mother's sister. Sadly, when we were there, she had recently passed away, but we met her husband, who was in his nineties. For some reason, Paul, who had been at school in Tientsin, also came to Macau to see father. Father went back to Kuala Lumpur, and the family, including Ching (who was nearly five, and who had lived up until now, in Kuala Lumpur with father), came back to Hong Kong.

It didn't seem like we had been back in Hong Kong for very long when mother got the news. Father had died. Cheng Yun Tin: July 14, 1890—February 25, 1941. As was the custom, we children were given the bare facts, and because we had been shifted around so much already, mother went alone to Kuala Lumpur for the funeral. War was a constant threat, and because she was worried about us, mother came home almost immediately. She would deal with the legalities of father's affairs later.

I didn't cry. I wouldn't let myself think about it. It wasn't difficult to pretend that father was in Kuala Lumpur still O.K. I had had to believe that, and pretend that, ever since I was five. Now, I can feel that five-year-old hug he gave me in 1930, when I first left him—it feels like he didn't want to let me go. Is he now punishing me for leaving him? I didn't realize then, that I was leaving my father's family—the Chengs, to go to my mother's family—the Kwans, and that I would be loved, cared for, shaped, influenced and guided by Kwans, and that father would always be far away. Is he now punishing me for my betrayal? I didn't know that our short time in Macau would be our last. I can't feel that goodbye hug. Was he refusing to let me hurt him once again? Or, when he was dying, was he calling out, asking me to forgive him for leaving me? Did he suffer? What did he look like? Was he at peace?

I wondered, I wondered, and all my question-mark tears will never be answered, ever. Now, the smell of wisteria will always set up in me, wistful feelings, vague longings, a deep emptiness—I will always miss my father. But, like everyone tells me, I must be big and brave, I must grow up. I will be my father's heroine. He can't go to war, so I must. I'll never watch that shadow-play of the make-believe heroine again. I've become her. Margeta came to find me, and we cried together. She told me that the dishes would always be special to her. A few days later, crates arrived from Kuala Lumpur—someone, having great kindness, had sent mother her bowls, spoons and all those soup tureens.

We took our lessons, with the master, on the all-purpose, perennials (soya and hot pepper sauces) removed, cloth covered, within ear-shot of Ah Dong's opened-door study, upstairs table. Today, we took our habitual places: I divided Kit and Mungie, and sat in full view of the study and the books lining its wall; Kit sat outside the view from the study, in a place where he could slip unnoticed under the cloth, if he had to save me from the "banging stick"; Betty, who was only there occasionally, sat next to Mungie, and coyly pestered him about taking her for a ride on the bicycle. They often went dual to young people's church outings: I don't know if she rode handle-bars, cross-bar, or rumble-seat; Cheuk and Chit sat together; if anyone else came, they could squeeze in beside Betty, so that all the cousins were a group. After the lesson, everyone dispersed, and left me sitting in place: I was looking at the colours and the arrangement of books on Ah Dong's shelves, and was imagining where he might place the "Kwan Book of Records", that he and Granduncle # 6 had started to compile, and now #6's son (I call him Uncle S.S.), mother and Ah Dong were trying to finish. Uncle S.S., who was a well established architect in mainland China and who (according to family stories) had an in with Chiang Kai-shek, was providing the financial support for the project, and had been. visiting here at the house recently, so the "Book" was on my mind. I found Uncle S.S.'s northern accent and mannerisms to be delightful. Kit, as was his duty, politely escorted the master down the stairs, and bowed him out the door. He quickly turned tail; bound up the stairs, two-steps-at-a-time; completely ignored me, still sitting at the table; went straight to Ah Dong and burst forth, "I don't believe what he said about the First Emperor, Qin!" And not even stopping for a breath, he went on, "No one would be so dumb!" Ah Dong, slowly and softly, asked Kit to go back down the stairs, and to come back up, and to enter his study with dignity and decorum. I could tell that Kit was furious. I didn't know that he had a double motive—a second agenda. He must have been thinking about it—what approach he would take—as he went down slowly, and came up just as slowly. I guess he decided to play his cards close and await an opportunity. "The master said that Qin in 221 B.C.E. united the provinces of China and formed the First Empire—The Qin Dynasty," he started and then continued, "The warlords of the provinces were very powerful, and constantly imperiled Qin's reign, and so, for protection, Qin surrounded himself with a great and powerful army.

He decreed that when he died, his army must be buried alive in his necropolis to protect him in the after-life. What Emperor would leave his country without an army? If this is just a legend, I don't see any sense in it. What is it suppose to teach?" Ah Dong was pleased. He had so often had to discipline Kit; he now took the opportunity to praise him: "Well done, Kit. That's precisely why you study history. It's supposed to make you think. If more people gave history some thought, maybe it wouldn't have to repeat itself." And then, without hesitation; seemingly, out of the blue, Kit said, "I want to join China's National Air Force." "Oh," was all that Ah Dong found to reply. And without letting Ah Dong say more, Kit went on, "I want to train to be a pilot. China's recruiting. Japan has been invading since '37, and China needs to build its forces. I think that now is the time—there's a good chance for me to be accepted. It's a perfect opportunity for me to get a career. After the war, I might be able to make a living flying. If not, I'm still young; I could go back to school later." "Hold on, hold on," Ah Dong was finally able to interject. "Take a breath."

I didn't realize that I had been holding mine. I didn't want to hear this conversation; maybe, I could faint.

"But, I think you need your high school diploma," came Ah Dong's voice from somewhere. And then, I heard: "Let's go talk to your mother and maybe to Grandpa. Perhaps, something can be arranged." Kit flew down the stairs, his feet sliding across the top of the steps, ignoring the indentations all together. Ah Dong went to the top, and was about to call after him about his un-decorous descent, but hesitated, and instead, just shook his head; turned to me, and said, "Such passion! Indeed, such passion! We mustn't discourage that kind of passion." He closed his study door, shutting in my imaginings, and went cautiously down the stairs, hanging securely onto the railing. I felt left behind: I felt those wistful stirrings in my gut—vague longings. The empty hole was expanding, and tears slid slowly over my cheeks, dripped onto my pages, and blurred my pomegranate doodles. The master had said that the emperor had a passion for pomegranates—he thought that the many seeds would be lucky, and would bring him many young soldiers. Maybe Kit could fly over China, spot the trees from above, and I could organize an expedition to exhume all those bones. That would answer all Kit's questions. After 2000-some-years, what would be left? I must be moonstruck—back in cloud cuckoo land.

On Saturday night, we dressed up, and went to # 107, which was the biggest Kwan house on Waterloo Road. It had been built on the same fashionable plans as the other two, but over the years it had taken on additions—one at the back and one on each side—wings. We called it the "landed airplane."

It not only had to house Granduncle and Grandaunt # 12's family, which included eight children, but it was also home to many Kwans, as they passed through Hong Kong, going here and there, all over the world—everyone was welcome at # 107. I wore the dress that Grandaunt # 11 had given me, when she left our house with her son, Uncle Y, and went to Tientsin to live with her other brother, Granduncle # 14. She had sewed the dress for herself, and was proud of her handiwork; so, it was extra special to me, and it now fit perfectly. The two Grandaunts (# 10 and # 11) often argued, which confused me. I think the gift was # 11's way of telling me, that she loved her sister, and I was not to worry over their petty misunderstandings. Anyway, when Cheuk, Margeta and I arrived, # 107 was already full of laughter and music and hospitality. Young people came early, bringing their musical instruments, or borrowed a pan to bang on, or they came to sing, or to just add to the laughter. Son # 5 (my Uncle Kun) was extremely musical: could play any instrument. Auntie Betty (# 8 and very close to my age) and # 6 would vie for the piano to show their talents, and we sang all the songs made popular by the movies, and danced to our heart's delight. Grandaunt # 12 would exaggerate her wiggle, as she balanced on very small feet—we would double over with laughter. There was a rule in the Mary Noll Convent—on Saturday nights all the windows on the Waterloo Road side were to be left opened to let in the happiness of music and laughter from # 107 across the street. The older ones came when they were free, but always made sure they were in time to eat. If you came to her house, Grandaunt # 12 expected to feed you—more rice could always be made, and another bowl could be put on the table. She was proud of the cuisine from her native village, and enjoyed having great pots of this food for people. Granduncle # 12 got down on the floor, and played marbles with Ching, who was disappointed to lose all his marbles, but we reassured him not to worry, Granduncle would wrap them up, and give them back to him as a Christmas present. You see, we knew the game; we had been in that same position ourselves, a few years back. And Granduncle talked to Mungie about going fishing after church tomorrow—there was a local creek, where they liked to take their luck. And then it was time to sing: "When I grow too old to dream, I'll have you to remember." That was always the goodnight song at # 107.

When we got home, Ah Dong, mother and Uncle Honkie sat for awhile, and talked about the "Book." Cheuk, Margeta and I sat on the carpet, chatting about the wonderful evening we had spent. Margeta asked about Grandaunt # 12's feet. Cheuk told us that binding young girl's feet was part of Chinese culture. That having "tiny feet" increased a girl's chances of marriage into a wealthy household, and girls with unbound feet would be consigned to the life of an old maid in their parent's home or a servant in someone else's. "Grandaunt # 12 was very proud of her bound tiny feet," Cheuk said. "She told me, that as part of her wedding dowry, a tailor came with her to her marriage home. He made beautiful slippers for her tiny feet, and embroidered them exquisitely.

And then, after the revolution, when China became a Republic, Granduncle # 12 operated on her feet to unbind them," Cheuk finished. "Why would he do that? And why would she let him?" asked Margeta. Mother had heard the conversation, and came to where we sat. "It wasn't just a cultural thing," she started. "It became, over the years, part of the culture, but it was a command from the Manchurian Imperial Government. It was a way of controlling the people. Young girls had to have their feet bound, and no boys could have their hair cut—they had to grow the que," mother said. "But why don't the other Grandaunts have small feet? Did Great Grandmother Kwan have small feet? How did she stand up in court with bound feet?" I asked. "You forget," mother said. "Great Grandmother was raised by the Cotswolds. No way would they have allowed their "daughter's" feet to be broken and bound, and with Great Grandmother's westernized thinking, no way would she have allowed that to happen to her daughters' feet." Ah Dong had been listening to the conversation, and he wanted to get some words in. "Yes, yes," he interrupted. "And you, Dai Day, your father, when he was in Chang Wong helping Dr. Sun, worked very hard, and they changed the law—the binding of feet and the que were no longer mandatory. They believed, that that; seemingly, small change, helped unite the country under the Republic more than a million propaganda issues could have done. It was like a forest fire out of control—most everybody welcomed the change. Your father made you proud of your big feet, Dai Day, and now you have a fetish for fashionable western shoes." "But why did Grandaunt # 12 let her husband operate on her feet," Margeta asked again. "Most of the Kwans embraced the consciousness of the new Republic, and wanted to participate in the changes," Ah Dong said. "But that's not the only reason that # 12 operated—he believed he could help his wife walk.

She went through excruciating pain, when her bones were broken and bound, and again, when they were re-broken and re-set, but you saw her tonight. Not only can she walk much better, but in her own fashion, she can even dance. And, if I'm going to church tomorrow; maybe, you'll dance me up the stairs, Honkie?" A bond was forming between father and son: they often discussed engineering and architectural problems concerning Honkie and Margeta's new home, well under construction. The years of separation were melting away. I didn't fear for my lost place in Ah Dong's affection: Ah Dong's heart just grew bigger with Honkie's homecoming—he was happier than I had ever seen him. Now that he was a Grandpa, that big heart just popped out of his chest, and he wore it on his sleeve. "In a moment, I'll take you up, but I would like to show you something. It's to hang in our new home." Honkie spoke while he was removing a painting from its crate. "A classmate owed me some money, and was unable to pay me, so he took this painting from his parent's collection. The artist is from Canada, and is little known. She came to London to study in 1899. She felt that the Royal Academy couldn't teach her how she wanted to paint Canadian landscapes, and she couldn't afford to frame them in the mandatory real gold leaf, so she shunned the Academy for other less prestigious schools.

I really like her interpretation of British Columbian forests. She has had successful showings in New York, Seattle, Vancouver, Victoria and Toronto. She is 70 years old. You know what they say about artists becoming famous after they die. I think I have a treasure. An original painting by Emily Carr might be worth a fortune someday." "Modern art confuses me," commented Ah Dong. "But hang it in your house, and invite me often to have a look at it. I think this one, I could come to appreciate." I thought that the trees looked magical. Maybe, one day, I could go and have a look at Emily's trees.

When I was feeling out-of-sorts, I didn't always escape to the wisteria. Sometimes, I just had to be in Grandauntie # 10's presence. She had a vibration about her—a high energy, if you will. She lifted me up. I often went to her room. It was simple, neat, tidy—uncluttered, sparsely furnished with a small wardrobe, single bed, one bedside table, beside which (but further back to the wall) a wash stand, with two dowels, holding linen towels, that hid whatever was on the two shelves behind. On the stand were matching, in beautiful blue porcelain, wash bowl, water jug and soap dish, which held sandalwood soap, that you could smell the minute you came into the room. In place of a chest, under the window which centered the outside wall, was a dual-purpose rather large but narrow desk, with two sets of drawers, one on each side. A short stack of books was at hand under the bedside table, as she often read in bed, bolstered against pillows and under the protection of a small wooden cross, the only adornment on that wall. Another small stack of books sat on the left side of the desk, near the edge and close to the back. Other books, I assumed, were in their places in the drawers. If her Bible wasn't open on the desk, it sat neatly on top of the other books. Next to the stack was a black-lacquered tray, covered with a broderie anglaise linen piece. A matching piece was under the blue Ginger-jar light on the bedside table. A thermos and two drinking cups sat on the tray. On the other side of the desk was an escritoire: it was exquisitely appointed with minute cuts of varying coloured woods that were inlayed to form an arrow pattern that edged the top and each side and outlined an elongated diamond in the middle of the top and on the front panel. In the center of the diamonds were inlays of mother-of-pearl. The key-hole on the front panel was fully exposed, as a mother-of-pearl tessera had been broken away. The key was kept inside the box in the pen holder, next to the ink well, opposite the stamp keeper. Grandauntie # 10 kept her special writings in the storage place under the writing surface. The box had belonged to her mother—my Great Grandmother Kwan. The Cotswolds had given it to her when she achieved her Nurse's Pin. When the Cotswolds returned to England, Great Grandmother and her "mother" wrote often to each other, and the letters were kept in the escritoire. Granduncle # 15 now has those letters and his mother's diaries. Dressed in dark western suits and ties and always with a black briefcase, he often comes here, to the house, to visit. He tells me that he has all the letters that his mother wrote to him when he was in Peking and all her personal correspondence in his briefcase, and that, he wants to publish them. I've heard some pretty outlandish stories about this Granduncle, so I'm a bit leery.

One story was about how he and other young revolutionists, carried away by Dr. Sun Yat Sen's passion and enthusiasm, tried to burn down the Imperial Palace, but failed. Luckily, his brother, Granduncle # 6, who was still the Imperial physician at the time, was able to save him from dire consequences. How did I get side-tracked? I was telling you about Grandauntie # 10's room. On the wall and separated by the desk and in the small allotted spaces left where the drapes ended, were framed pictures of the Blue Boy and the Matching Girl. They would have to look across the simmering sea of blue brocade to even get a glimpse of each other.

The visitor's chair, which had its seat and back rest in the same brocade, stood, elegantly, on Queen Anne legs, by the door. The other furnishings exposed, to varying degrees, the same legs, except the desk which was, by all accounts, much more modest.

When I went to her room, Grandauntie # 10 was out. Apparently, she had gone, around by the Garden Triangle, down the street, to her house that she lets out, to give her financial independence. Her maid was expecting her home soon, so I sat on the bed to wait. It must have felt "just right" as I lay down, and was soon fast asleep. I dreamt that the Blue Boy came across the sea; took the Matching Girl's hand, and they came, and placed themselves together, on the wall, above the elegant chair, by the door.

When Grandauntie # 10 returned, we took hot water from the thermos, and I asked her if she was happy living the single life. She looked at me rather quizzically; as if, she wondered where that question came from, and she spoke: "For as long as I can remember, everyday, even as a young girl, I've asked for divine guidance, and I've listened for it, and I've expected it to come. It doesn't come; necessarily, how I expect it, but over the years, I've followed, and I've had a wonderful life of Joy, Love, and Peace. It's not an easy life—it took many years to realize that turmoil, conflict, agitation, disorder and chaos are not compatible to living in-spirit. By in-spirit, I mean: Realizing that I am a part of God and that I should struggle to live from that part of me and not from my ego self—from the material me. To do that effectively, it's imperative that I live a simple, uncluttered life. If you read my book marks, you'll see that I'm reminded constantly what Socrates wrote: 'I've lived long enough to learn how much there is that I can really do without . . . He is nearest to God who needs the fewest things'." "I understand that, Grandauntie # 10, but surely, that doesn't mean that you couldn't have married?" "Oh that," she said. "That was probably the greatest divine intervention of my entire life." "Oh?" "You see, Sister # 11, came into my life to teach me many things," she started. "My marriage had been arranged, and when the wedding day came, mother was very ill. She had been failing for some time, but on that day, she became critical. The wedding sedan, carrying my future husband, whom I had never met, as was the custom, was on its way to our house to take me to his.

I was dressing in my marriage costume, and I looked up to be a moment with God, and immediately I knew, without any doubts, that I wasn't going to go. Sister #11, who was helping me dress, didn't quite know what was taking place, when I convinced her to put on the marriage costume.

She climbed into the sedan, and married the unsuspecting groom, and I remained at home to nurse mother. Nursing mother and being with her through her dying days and when she passed over were profound, loving, spiritual experiences that I don't believe any marriage could ever match. I was honoured to have shared enlightening moments with the mother who had been my inspiration. And, Sister # 11 had a happy marriage, and she conceived your Uncle Y almost immediately. But, Sister # 11 wasn't through with me yet. You see, her husband died before your Uncle Y was born, and probably, because of unhappiness and stress and youth and vanity, she blamed me. She said that I had given her "a dead cat," and we had great arguments over it. She taught me that that kind of bedlam moved me away from the life that I was trying to devote myself to. When I learnt the lesson, we were at peace, and she and Uncle Y happily moved north to live with Brother # 14, who had been asking her to come for some time. She gave you her beautiful dress. She had trained, and had become a mid-wife: she wanted to be of service—not a spoiled show-piece. She had become a Kwan—mother would have been proud of her." I don't know what it was, it's not something that you can put your finger on and say: "Eureka", but I know, that somehow, I had learnt something today. In our family, we don't show physical affection easily: to hug Grandauntie # 10 would have embarrassed both of us, so I put my hands together, and gave a slight hint of a bow, and thanked her for sharing her story with me. I don't think that she had planned to do so, and I was noticeably touched, and had to quietly take leave from her room—it was now, even more dear to me.

Another school year was about to begin, and Ah Dong had instructed us to design our new school bags, and he would have the rag man sew them. Cousin Gay, Auntie Violet's oldest son (one of seven boys) had come from Shanghai sometime after the Japanese invasion there in '37, and he lived here with us. He had special instructions from Ah Dong, that this year, he must be more careful with his design. There are so many Kwan relatives, and it's interesting how children are shifted back and forth amongst them—parents are always trying to find the best education, appropriate opportunities or they are just trying to keep the children out of harm's way. For examples, Cousin Gay now lives with us, and I, at one time, lived with his family. In '32 mother took Cheuk, Chit and me to Shanghai to school. Cheuk and Chit weren't happy there, so Cheuk came back to Ah Dong's and Chit went home to her parents in Kaula Lumpur, and I stayed, under the guardianship of Auntie Violet, in Shanghai.

Shanghai went from being a small fishing village to being the "Paris of the East." When the Dowager Queen rebelled (Boxer Rebellion) against foreign aggression, foreign troops retaliated, and took over Peking.

In the peace terms, the Dowager didn't have black birds in her pie, but she had black pearls (all the ports and the rights for foreign trade—tea, silk, and porcelain for opium), and she cut the pie into pieces, and gave it to France, Britain and the U.S. Shanghai got cut into concessions and each was ruled by a foreign country. As a consequence, Shanghai was booming in growth, business, schools, churches and in every other thinkable aspect. Our families—the Kwans, the Yungs, the Kans and other branches—flocked there to make money, for education, to start churches, or just to be where all the action was. It was the "in" place, and even as a child, I was impressed—I was in this most sophisticated school. But, when Shanghai was deemed unsafe, I too came back to Ah Dong's.

I remember that school year when Cousin Gay was first with us. His ink bottle didn't have a proper compartment in his school bag, or he never closed the lid tightly. He would arrive home with blue blotches all over his white uniform. And, because he always pushed and shoved to be the first off the bus, he would fall down the steps, and land in the dirt: he would not only be blue, but he would also be black. Ah Dong wanted an explanation, and we answered, that it was because of Cousin Gay's "Big Head." He was top heavy, and took to falling over. Ah Dong didn't take kindly to this explanation, and we all had our turn in the time-out-thinking-chair. Cousin Gay must come home looking respectable.

School started, and we settled into our routine—school, church, young peoples, occasional dinner out for special occasions, Saturday nights at # 107, sessions with the master, piano lessons, the annual visit to the "Blind School" and study, study, study. And, oh yes, All Saint's Day visit to clean the cemetery is coming up soon.

On Sundays, mother drove to church. She was one of only a few women who drove: she was a competent driver, and enjoyed the trip. We went over to Hong Kong side by ferry, then up to the Mid-levels, somewhere by Kennedy Street, not far from the "Tram," that goes up to the Peak. We referred to it as Ah Dong's Church, but officially, I think it is called The Union Church or in Chinese, Hop Yat Tong. Mother has told me that families or their children, who were members of this church, have moved to all parts of the world. Someone might be in Australia, or in the U.S., or in Canada for instance, and chances are, they'll meet someone with connections back to Hop Yat Tong. The church is like a home-anchor for many people. Ah Dong is an elder, and he serves at the communion table during the Chinese service. We children don't like to go to both the English and the Chinese services, so sometimes we get to go up the "Tram" to visit mother's Brother # 6 and his family. He maintains the Communications Tower on the Peak, and being isolated, his children sometimes have to stay with relatives down in Kowloon or Hong Kong.

We have a glorious time running around the Peak with all our cousins. Often, on school holidays, we get to stay for a few days—those are very happy times.

On All Saint's Day, November 1st, Grandauntie # 10, arranged for our annual visit to the cemetery. The day was warm, and she had brought a picnic lunch that we would have, under the trees, behind, after our work was finished. We swept, and cleaned, and polished, and re-finished letterings and placed bouquets of flowers on many grave sites. Great Grandfather and Great Grandmother Kwan's large orange-brown marble marker had all their fifteen children's names carved on it: the birth dates were in place and the death dates would be added in time. It struck me that in life, death is a given—the timing all depends on when someone might carve the second set of numbers into the stone. And, the—between the birth and death numbers was so short. Life was a fleeting affair. I learnt that Grandaunt # 1, who they said was the prettiest daughter, lived fifty-one years, and Grandaunt # 5, who I've already told you, tutored English to her brothers and to Dr. Sun Yat Sen, and who they said was the most brilliant, lived only thirty-four years, and Granduncle # 4 lived only a short time—four months. I actually liked going to the cemetery and looking at the different types of markers—how they changed in design over the years. I pondered over names and dates, and wondered how people might have lived, and how they died; especially, when I noticed a very short life. I remembered being told that the Governor General had organized a small marching band to accompany Great Grandmother's casket to this burial ground. There must have been only a trail leading up this very steep hill to the site. I could imagine the French horn player, trying to look dignified, blowing and puffing his way up. I wondered when the great orange-brown marble marker was brought up here and put in place. Was Great Grandmother honoured with it, or was she marked with a humble cross, and made to wait until Great Grandfather died, to have her numbers carved in stone. All the lettering was the same style, and all had aged the same. Ah Dong nor Grandauntie # 10, much to my surprise, could remember that kind of detail. If a grave looked neglected, I borrowed a few of our flowers to place on it. I hoped that the deceased would feel remembered.

During our picnic Ah Dong would tell us stories—usually something from the past that the visit had piqued to memory. But, today he wanted to talk about Kit. "I'm so proud of Kit," he said. "Kit explained to us, how we had taught him to be proud of his country and its long history of great achievements. History taught him that Japan wasn't going to be satisfied with just having Taiwan—they wanted all of South-East Asia. He was adamant that we had to fight. If we didn't, he swore that we would be prisoners in our own country—we would be Chinese in a Japanese cangue. 'And,' he said, 'This war is going to be won from the air. Aviation's time has come, and I must be a part of it.' He was full of passion." "Just the fact that he was interested and excited about doing this, is all the evidence he needed—inspiration was right in front of him, begging him to pay attention.

Maybe that's why he incarnated in the first place—he might have been remembering his purpose," spoke Grandauntie # 10. "We must all keep him in our prayers."

Life and its routine went on, and now we could start looking forward to Christmas. We would have holidays from school, pageants and plays and Christmas songs at church; and of course, we all looked forward to the presents, tucked under the blanket, around the tree, at Ah Dong's house—Ching, for sure, would get his marbles back from Granduncle # 12. There were constant air raid sirens, but they were always false alarms—we paid little heed.

Then, one morning, December 12th, 1941, our routines came to a full stop. We were on our way to school (the sirens were on as usual), and suddenly, we saw hundreds of planes in the sky. We could see the "red sun" painted on the wings; we could see bombs dropping. We were mesmerized. We pointed and shouted, "Look over there!" "Over there!" "Over there!" I remember the smoke, but mostly, I remember the noise: low flying planes; sirens (seemingly from everywhere now); people hollering, yelling and screaming: "Run!" "Run!" "Run!" We paid no heed to Ah Dong's warning that we bring Cousin Gay home looking respectable—we dragged him, and ran.

Mother was resigned. There had been, for so long, too much nervous anticipation. All she said was, "So it finally happened." Somehow, I think she felt relief. She probably had plans in her mind, and she could now take action. She was calm, but no one could miss that she was a determined women—a force to be reconciled with. She mustered up as much help as she could, took me, and went to all the small neighbourhood grocery shops. She bought as many canned goods as we could handle—as far as her money would go. We got home to discover that there was no water: the reservoir had been targeted. We should have bought bottled drinks as well. Next, she prepared the attic. The attic was below the roof and above Ah Dong's study—the place where Kit and Ah Soh would hide to work on their "projects." The only access was by rope ladder. Somehow, we got mattresses, blankets, utensils, lanterns and all things mother thought necessary, up the ladder, and when the time came, all women and children would sleep in the attic. The next thing, I think, she found the most difficult. She gathered the servants, and dismissed them to go home to their families. King King, the most senior and most faithful, refused to leave. She remained with mother.

All men (all ages, all walks of life), from field workers, store helpers, company owners and professionals, were on duty alert—all volunteers. In the event of an attack, they were to aid the British Defense Units. The concentration was aimed to protect the Hong Kong harbour—certainly attackers would come that way. A Japanese battle ship "The Sun Rise," anchored out beyond the Hong Kong legal water zone, had been there so long, it was considered a "warning" rather than a "threat." As it turned out, it was a stalking horse—a decoy. The Japanese attack, that fateful December morning, was a surprise: they flew their planes through a narrow passage up by Lions Mountain, directly into Kowloon Tong.

A week passed; mother was now prepared. Everything; however, seemed quiet. There had been no more bombings. Maybe, the attack had been just a warning: the Japanese were not going to invade after all. Life could go back to routine.

Then, the rude awakening came. Not in ones wildest imaginings, could this be considered routine. It was four o'clock in the morning (the time is etched on my mind); there came a loud banging at the door. Mother and I quickly dressed, and holding hands, opened. With bloodied swords drawn, there stood three bloodied Japanese soldiers. Mother was calm: appeared as if the sight we faced was nothing unusual. She picked up a pencil and pad, and asked what they might want. They answered by walking directly into the house. One was in command: he had many stars—high ranking, we assumed. And, through the still open door, we could hear mostly, and see a little, horses stomping and soldiers making a raucous.

They had come to take a census—at four o'clock in the morning?—all bloodied from killing. The pencil and paper went back and forth, "How many men? How many women? How many children?" "12" "Only see 3" "Upstairs" "Why?" "It is night." "Must come down. Must line up." "Only see 10." "2 invalids—can not do stairs." The commando pointed his sword at Cousin Cheuk (she was seventeen or eighteen and very beautiful), and gestured for her to get him a drink of water. "No water—bottled drink O.K.?" You must realize that Cousin Cheuk was a very spoiled young lady: she was used to having a maid, and besides, King King was right here. Mother spoke to her in Chinese, "Pour the drink into a good glass; serve it on a tray." The commando signaled for Cheuk to take a drink: he wasn't taking any chances. He then wanted to tour the house. Mother obliged him, and led the way. In Ah Dong's house the Japanese custom of removing your outside shoes and putting on slippers was strictly enforced. Ironically, in this Chinese house, the Japanese soldiers forgot all about their own custom, and stomped up the stairs in their muddy boots. Their black tracks, smudged with red, followed conspicuously, behind them. I half expected Ah Dong to send them back down to remove their boots and to come up with dignity, as he had done so many times with Kit. Singularly, the tracks up the stairs looked like a mess to be cleaned up, but as a unit and from my perspective (from a distance and from the bottom looking up), they were the dunnocks, their wings shot through with a twinge of red, lifting up in unison from the peach tree, when Ah Soh was on save-the-fruit patrol.

The unruly commando that went up the stairs wasn't the same man that came down. His sword was in its sabretache, and he gingerly attempted to step on the same dunnocks, so as not to add anymore to the flock. Mother told me that when he went into Grandauntie # 10's room something happened to him. Grandauntie # 10 had been reading her Bible; she looked up at him and smiled. He wrote on the pad, "My grandmother—She a Christian." He bowed, and backed politely out of the room.

He came down the stairs, and then, quite graciously, made everything perfectly clear. He would allow: all members of the household to remain upstairs; King King, once a day, at his designated time, to go to the kitchen for food; all windows to be blacked out. The Japanese were taking over our house and the Kowloon Tong Club next door for their Headquarters. What would have happened to us, if he was the same commando that first came into the house? Immediately, the fence came down between the two buildings, and the cavalry allowed their horses to stomp Ah Dong's precious grasses to a muddy mess. Over night, a mighty lookout tower was erected on the grounds.

Apparently, during the week of devious calm, the Japanese infiltrated all of Kowloon Tong and Hong Kong. In this bloody night of terror, they made their invasion known: Hong Kong and Kowloon Tong were occupied territories. The lookout towers sprung up everywhere—we were being watched. Ah Dong's beloved church was converted into a tower. Was God watching them watch us? We had to get permission; we had to get permission; we had to get permission—if we wanted to breathe, we had to get permission. And, there was a shortage of everything; especially, food and water. People were starving: corpses were everywhere. In the morning, trucks came by to clear the streets.

The Japanese were an organized lot: they took a census—everyone was registered (had to carry a card); they set up rice stations—each person was allowed three ounces (one sixteenth of a pound, twenty eight grams, one very small amount) of rice per day. They needed Chinese people who could read and write to man these stations, and to keep records. Mother, always alert to seize an opportunity, offered Betty and me—I wasn't pretty—I shouldn't have any problems with the menacing soldiers.

It was horrible! I was a young teenager (who should have been in school); instead, I was maneuvering around dead or dying bodies trying to get to the rice station. If I closed my eyes, or covered my nose and mouth from the stench, I might trip over a protruding leg or a rogue arm. Some bodies were quartered or carved, and meat was missing—food for the hungry: "God, what a dreadful time to be alive." I let my mind go from these sights. My thoughts ran to Ah Dong, Grandaunt # 10, Granduncle and Grandaunt # 12, Grandpa, mother and my brothers. I must get the rice and my daily wage—one Japanese military note. On occasion, I could buy stolen tin goods from the soldiers, and some one could get them into the concentration camp. That's where foreigners were placed. I knew that some of my former teachers and friends from Mary Noll Convent were there. I was worried about Margeta. They had moved from Ah Dong's into their own house, and keeping in contact was difficult. I know that she eventually went home to England, but I don't know how or when, exactly.

The Japanese also controlled our access to the banking system: we were allowed fifteen dollars withdrawal per month: our safety deposit boxes had to be opened in front of an armed officer: every item was meticulously recorded: we could remove nothing. Strangely, one day mother was summoned by the commando (who had made the four o'clock in the morning visit) to open her safety deposit box. He wanted to buy her diamond ring and earrings. These had been willed to her from her mother—a wedding gift from my grandmother's Hawaiian parents. I don't remember the exact offer—maybe three thousand or maybe it was five thousand. Mother thought it was a "Rainfall," a "Blessing from God;" besides, the money was in Japanese military notes!

After that transaction, things changed: The Japanese left our house, and occupied only the Club; yellow banners (signed by the commando) went up around our property—no soldiers could trespass; King King and Mungie could have the yard for a garden (they planted much needed vegetables). The commando was once again showing his humanity. I believe, that he was touched by Grandauntie # 10's spirit and, that he was thankful to be able to buy mother's diamonds. The whole family thought, that life might have been much different, if it wasn't for this particular commando.

Grandauntie # 10's health deteriorated. My # 3 Uncle (from granduncle # 9) and # 10 Uncle (from Granduncle # 2)—both medical doctors—risked passing Japanese blockades to come to attend her. They trained mother to do the nursing, and they instructed me in basic care-giving for the dying. Together, we lovingly bathed, changed, fed and turned her. We plumped pillows and changed bedding and opened and closed those blue drapes over and over—anything, if it would make her more comfortable, and she never once complained. Her legs and feet would be cramped up tight, and she let me massage them with lavender oil, and she was thankful. Near the end her voice was but a mere whisper, but her hearing was good, and she appreciated it, if we read from her Bible. Being with her, I remembered what she had told me about her own mother's dying. Now, I understood. The commando sent six Japanese soldiers to accompany her casket to the burial ground. He had had only one very brief encounter with her—that night that he came to take over our house. Watching her respectful Japanese escort, how could I not believe, that she had touched him in a very special way?

Rules changed, and now, people were allowed to evacuate to the mainland. This last initiative would decrease the island population: it would be easier for the Japanese to manage. Uncle Honkie took the children (a son, David and a baby daughter, Nancy) and left.

Mother felt responsible for so many people. She was determined to protect us all. She certainly wasn't going to let us starve. The small amount of rice we got was almost always old, often gritty, sometimes moldy, exceptionally smelly, and occasionally had worms—the extra protein was welcome. After the house was returned to us, and we felt somewhat safe (what with the yellow banners), and the garden started producing, mother turned her mind to (what she considered) other basic things. You see, education was in the Kwan family motto: it was genetic: it held high priority. Mother was worried, that I was missing very important years of my education, and, as I have told you, when she saw an opportunity, she seized it. She had heard that a group of missionaries was evacuating to the interior of the mainland. I must go with them. She had allocated a part of her "diamond money" and she had made arrangements. "Why me"? I begged. "No!" "Not me!" But, mother had given it much thought. Father was dead. She hadn't heard from Paul or Kit—she assumed, that they were still in China. She had to make decisions. Who knew how long this war would drag on? Cousin Cheuk would have to stay under mother's care: she was responsible for her, and would have to answer to Cheuk's father (her Brother #2, my Uncle Kin Tong), if anything should happen to her. Mother had another argument, and this was meant to end the confrontation. "Besides," she said, "Every night, I hear you screaming with terrifying nightmares." I answered: "I do not cry anymore. I'm used to the conditions." Mother would have the last word, "All the more reason," she explained gently and very quietly, so I would be sure to hear, "If you see suffering, and can not shed a tear, then you have lost all reason to be alive." And then, in case I might come up with something else, she quickly said, "Besides, we need Mungie to do the garden."

Mother was given permission to exchange a limited amount of Japanese military notes into Chinese dollars. This money, plus the rest of the "diamond money", that was allocated for me, was given to mother's friend, Mrs. Lien. She was the missionary's organist. On this mission, she had in tow, not only my money, but also, a large portable organ. The group that I was to join consisted of: five senior pastors; ten recently graduated Bible School students; Mrs. Lam (a matron); and Mrs. Lien. I was entrusted to one of the pastors. He should leave me at the first Christian school we came to, that he deemed safe.

I had said goodbye to my father, when I left Kuala Lumpur in 1930, and again, when I said my last goodbye to him in Macau in 1938. I had said goodbye to Ah Dong, Grandpa and the others, when I went to Shanghai in 1932. All these goodbyes, in no way, prepared me for this one. Before, there had always been hugs, smiles, good lucks and good wishes. There was sadness at leaving, but there was also some excitement about going on a new journey. This time, the sadness was impossible to bear. Grandaunt # 10 had recently died, Ah Dong was quiet, Granduncle and Grandaunt # 12 simply shook their heads, unable to speak, and Grandpa was in shock. "How could you make such a decision?" he spoke directly at mother. "She is merely fifteen—too young—too immature—how can you send her off to no-man's-land? We have no idea, if the conditions there are better than here, or worse," he said, his voice rising. "Besides," he ranted, "There won't be a Kwan in sight to help her." Silence went round the room—shouting. He turned to me, "I don't have any money, but if your mother insists on this plan, I have something you must take." He gave me a very large bottle of sulfanilamide (a recently discovered drug: effective against some infections). It had been given to him as a sample. His doctor's voice returned, "It might help you or others, take care of it." I should have felt some relief: I was escaping from horrific Hong Kong. What I really felt was raw, absolute fear.

Mother managed by keeping busy—she always took action; the missionaries were leaving almost immediately. She packed everything she thought essential into a huge trunk. She knew that she had upset her father, so; of course, she lovingly included "the medicine." She thought of it as a "forgiveness gift"—she knew her father wouldn't hold a grudge. He would understand (when he calmed down) that she was only doing what she thought was best for me.

Mother gave me my British Passport and a Bible that she recently had re-covered in leather. She took back my "black book" (a birth certificate that recorded place, date, time; was used, as was the Chinese custom, to astrologically guide ones future). I had had it with me since my school stay in Shanghai. "You don't need this," she said. "All you need is yourself and the presence of God." I struggled. I dug deep in my memory box to try and find what Ah Dong had taught me about courage. I managed to say goodbye to mother. With her blessing and her very heavy trunk, I boarded the refugee boat. I wasn't thinking about whether or not I had the courage or the wisdom to face the challenges that awaited me. I was too busy biting my lip to keep it from trembling and squeezing my eyes tight to hold in the tears.

We sailed by day, making sure to be anchored in some safe port before nightfall. We might go ashore, stretch our legs, and perhaps stop at a tea shop, savour a local pastry. The boat's cook often had freshly caught fish or newly picked vegetables, so we were eager to be back on board to take our evening meal.

We reached Kwan Chow Bay (a small port in Fukien Province), and disembarked. This place was bustling, thriving: many refugees came through here. There was plenty of information to be had; countless number of willing guides; all sorts of sedans or carrying carts to let. My Japanese military notes felt their worth in this "open-for-business" harbour: Mrs. Lien was able to obtain six or eight (I don't remember exactly) commodity certificates in Chinese dollars. She reasoned that I would need at least five years of schooling, and, that we should stretch each certificate out for at least a year—to be on the safe side.

Our group left Kwan Chow Bay on foot; headed toward the remote western part of China. We took pathways, over the mountains, from one village to the next. Only small sedans or single-wheeled carts could pass through the narrow trails. The missionaries had a vague plan, and had some idea as to the route they were going to take. You see, the London Missionary Society had been in China since 1805—the same group that had converted those first ten Chinese (including my Great, Great Grandfather) to Christianity. They had started a number of projects throughout this area. Because of the war, many projects were in disarray. The missionaries that had been working there were forced to abandon them. This group wanted to visit some of these projects: wanted to revitalize them, or in someway, to offer help. On their list was a school for the blind, an orphanage and a clinical station.

Walking all day, carrying as much as possible, or pushing the over-loaded carts up hill, or controlling them from running away down hill, was not easy. We all were out of shape, and were under nourished from living in Hong Kong. Luckily, the weather was pleasant and the villages were quaint and interesting. Even in the smallest "inns," the people were hospitable, and although humble, the places were always clean. We ate a lot of fresh vegetables and fruit, which was a Godsend, and we didn't have any trouble falling asleep, even if the mattress was of straw. And, nobody complained. Far be it for me not to follow suit. Eventually, we reached their first destination—the "Blind School." Mrs. Hu, who we called Mama, was in charge. We all pitched in. Mountains of vegetables were preserved; stacks of bean curd were fermented; the cold cellar was piled high. We scrubbed and cleaned (not only the building, but the children, as well)—their bodies and their souls. Local help was instructed: they would carry on when we left.

I was comfortable with the blind children. They loved to sing; I taught them new songs which they translated into Braille. It touched me to watch them earnestly recording: "This Little Light of Mine." How does a light shine, for one who does not see?

When I was here, I couldn't help, but think of Ah Dong. He tried to teach us "Charity." His annual project was to take us up the hill next to the Dairy Farm (the one with the Mandarin ducks), to the Blind School. As gifts, we had to take something that belonged to us—a pencil, a note book, perhaps a toy. Ah Dong, mother and Grandauntie # 10 would load the car with fruit. It always surprised me. When the children touched us, they could remember our names. They would entertain with "performing arts"—a small play, a few songs. And, we in turn, must perform for them. Kit was in his element: he often went to the Chinese Opera with King King: he liked music, he loved acting. I remember one time he practiced for months jumping around like the "Monkey King." Much to his chagrin, the blind children couldn't see his polished antics. However, the day was saved: they loved it, when he sang "like an opera star." We were all treated to ice cream from the Dairy Farm.

Then, the day came, and the missionaries deemed that their work was done, so we said our goodbyes, and left the "Blind School." The first day on the road, I was very quiet. I was saddened by having to say goodbye yet again, and I was constantly thinking about Grandauntie # 10. It surprised me that I couldn't conjure up her face—I could hear lots of her words, but I didn't have a picture of her in my mind. I had spent so much time with her. How could this happen? I didn't dare try to see my father's face—I had to trust that it would be there. I wasn't ready to lose him—completely. It wasn't very long until we were travelling through Kung Ting Wu, the "Rice Bowl of China." Here, the people seemed to be better off—not so poor. I remember walking around the lake. We could see the boatmen dressed in Sanfoos—all pink and green. Their singing followed us on our way.

When we reached Kwangsi province, it was the Dumpling Festival. Some Christian families invited us aboard their houseboats; treated us to the most delicious dumplings. It made me think of the wonderful wedding dinner Ah Dong had given Honkie and Margeta and the special winter melon soup we had and how Grandpa had told me that I was part Hawaiian and how happy I was. Watching the fireflies and the moon shining on the water, and being satiated, and being rocked by the houseboat, I forgot the gruesome starvation I had experienced in Hong Kong.

We noticed, as we travelled further into the interior, that the people seemed to be getting poorer and poorer: they eked out a living on every available bit of land. We watched the farmers irrigating their crops. They pedaled a contraption (like a bicycle) that turned a water wheel. We could hear them joking and laughing as they went about their work. Perhaps, they were laughing at us: the toilets were very public. The toilet was a small hut (on stilts) in the middle of a man-made lake. Narrow wooden walkways led to this "privacy." Domestic animal wastes also went into these lakes, and many fish were added to produce fertilizer. Gas, generated from this mess, lit their huts. And, who could forget the toilet paper? I had lived with the niceties at Ah Dong's; I had lived in sophisticated Shanghai. This "paper" was handmade; had visible and very palpable dried straw. I gathered soft leaves to complement this rough brown-yellow "scratch."

Then, we started entering the mountainous regions of Kwei Chow, and began noticing different minority groups, and realized that opium was becoming more and more prevalent; as were beggars—young boys followed us, they hung around. Finally, we came to the Mission Orphanage. The main stream here was young boys—street kids (abandoned). Their crimes fed their bellies and their opium addiction. Maybe the ones that ended up in the orphanage were lucky: others went to reform school or to some other kind of prison. Probably, any one of the three was a Hell on earth. I knew what it felt like to be invaded. These kids had it far worse: they no longer owned their human dignity.

The orphanage didn't have enough food. It certainly didn't know how to deal with drug addiction. It would lock the kids in; give them a bed; teach them morality; save their souls. For my part (and I'm embarrassed to even tell you about it), I told them a Chinese version of the stories about Cinderella and Little Red Riding Hood. Where, in these childish tales, on an empty stomach, could hardened kids (much older than their years) find morality?—of any kind. At night, I redeemed myself: I unlocked the door, and let them out to steal food. In August, we heard that the farmers needed extra hands for harvesting. The missionaries allowed me to take a band of boys. We worked hard together, and were given food for pay. One day the farmer brought us a big hat full of peaches, and told us to take a break, under a tree, in the shade. My mouth watered at even the thought of the peaches. I was remembering my favorite tree in Ah Dong's garden. A young boy, being food savvy, showed me how to rub off the little fuzz that there was, and then he ate his peach with pleasure and abandon. When I bit into mine, I noticed that the flesh wasn't golden, but was more a whitish-pale-yellow, and it wasn't sweet and soft, and no juices ran down my arms, to be licked off. I didn't try to explain to my fellow workers, that I was a spoiled brat, and in my youth, peaches were sweet, and life was good. We pitched hay up high on to carts; we slashed corn from their stalks; we picked late fruit, and we ate well, and grew strong. I tried to teach the boys what Grandma Kwan had taught me about leaving some fruit on the tree to assure a good crop next year. They joked among themselves, and laughed at my "airy-fairy" ideas. "Make sure you leave it low down on the tree," they said, being always practical. "To night we'll come back and fill our bellies." It was good to hear their laughter, and I hoped that life could go on like this forever for the boys, but I knew harvest would soon be over, and, as for them, they would again be tattered by the winds.

As for me, mid-September came, and the pastor, to whom I had been entrusted, thought it was time to find me a school. After we left the orphanage, he started making inquiries in the villages on our route. As it happened, one day we took lunch under a grove of trees. Much to my delight, I discovered that the trees were pomegranates. I took it to be a prophecy: I wasn't meant to go to school. I was meant to stay right here and dig. I explained the story of Emperor Qin to my travelling companions. I think the pastor thought that I was half serious about staying here, so he gave me a po-faced look, and said that it was a most entertaining lunch-time story, and that he had a story of his own to tell: He had learned of a Christian school that was housed in a temple, high up in the mountains. The United Christian High School found safe haven, high above the mid-stream of the Yangtze River, in a Ming dynasty built hermitage. I explained to him that that all sounded very nice, but I had grown strong doing the farm chores, and now I found it much easier to travel—I was quite enjoying the nomadic life. I was sure that there would be another school further along the way. He reminded me what he had promised mother, and he said, "A promise is a promise. This is the first Christian school that we have come to that appears plausible." If the truth be known, I didn't want to leave these kind caring missionaries. They often told me that I was like a daughter to them—they had become family. I couldn't possibly say another goodbye. Father had left me, Paul and Kit had left me, Grandauntie # 10 had left me, and I had left all the others that I loved back in Hong Kong—Mother, Mungie, Ching, Grandpa and Grandma, Granduncle and Grandaunt # 12, and my dear Ah Dong, who was aging. And I didn't know how many cousins were still there. When I thought of Kit, I wondered where he might be. After basic training (square-bashing), if he was accepted into the flying squadron, he would likely go to India for pilot training. No matter how I protested, it was decided that tonight would be my last with them, and tomorrow the pastor and I would make the climb up to the school. Overwhelmed with every kind of emotion, in a strange bed, late that night, in secrecy, I wept my shameful tears into a hay-smelling strange pillow. And, I forgot, what I had been told, over and over, since I was a small child of five leaving my father for the first time: "Be big and brave and don't cry."

So, with the trunk that mother had packed for me and the remaining Chinese dollar commodity certificates, it was here, that I was left. The temple, sheltered by many old trees and shrubs, was majestic. The people, from the valleys below, had been climbing up the two hundred and eighty steps, for hundreds of years, to worship here. They left chou sticks and oil in the lamps. There was no running water, no electricity and no glass in the windows. We had the outside barrels, oil lamps and rice paper in place of glass. The temple was certainly not hermetically sealed. It was drafty, and in winter, it could be bitter cold. We wore many layers, and carried bamboo heaters (woven baskets with a clay bowl to hold charcoal). The monks were most kind. They carried themselves with so much dignity, and willingly served their religion and the school. Giving up their sleeping quarters for the students, they moved into a small shed, and they climbed up and down those many steps, many times, carrying water for our barrels.

I didn't adapt easily to my new school. I missed my travelling companions terribly, and didn't want to make new friends—once again, and I was often frustrated. It was; mostly, the language that caused me problems. I spoke Cantonese, Shanghai dialect and pigeon English. Mandarin was difficult: my tongue wouldn't curl around these new sounds. And, much to my chagrin, everyone called me "Little Cantonese." I knew why the name bothered me so much. When I was in grade school, shortly after arriving in Kowloon Tong, from Kuala Lumpur, I was bullied because of my name. My name sounded like a word, that wasn't very nice, and the other kids called me by the not-nice-name. To make things worse, Cousin Cheuk's name was very nice, and I was always compared to her. So, mother, being mother, took action. She legally changed my name; I became Man Sheung. This has to be the longest, most complex name to be written in Chinese characters—mother said that no one could possible shorten it to anything nasty, and she was right. In time the not-nice-name was forgotten, and the new name garnered great respect. And, it took me many hours of practice before I could write my new name—in frustration it's a wonder that I didn't shorten it, myself.

So, at this school, which was basic, to say the least, and where communication was difficult, and the cacophony of foreign sounds screamed at me, and where I was bullied by a name that poked fun at me, I, most often, would just shut out my surroundings and all the sounds, and let myself daydream. Off my mind would go to my sophisticated school in Shanghai: I had been a younger student, but in my dreams, I became a senior—all glamorous, fashionable and famous. I thought of all the relatives that I had met when I was in Shanghai and the lifestyle that they lived—it certainly was grand compared to what I've known since. I often visited my Aunt (her father was Granduncle #2) and Uncle in Soo Chow—we refer to them as our Soo Chow relatives. Their son, my cousin Hey, I came to know very well, as he helped me with my homework, and he was often at Soo Chou Aunt # 7's, when I spent school breaks with her. She was a high school teacher, and was single, and had time, and was very congenial with young people, so we all flocked to her. Soo Chou Aunt # 10 was a nursery teacher in Shanghai, who always thought that she had to feed me, so when I wanted dumplings, I visited her. Surprisingly, her dumplings didn't come to mind, when I was on the house boat, during Dumpling Festival. Her dumplings were; probably, every bit as good as the ones we enjoyed there, but the circumstances made the house boat dumplings special. A number of the Soo Chou aunts escaped the Japanese invasion in '37 and went to Hong Kong—the same time that I went back to Ah Dong's. And; of course, I spent a lot of time at Auntie Violet and Uncle Lin's house with the seven boy cousins. Uncle Lin, an eye surgeon, was busy with his practice, but when he was home, he always had time for us, and he was very jolly. Auntie Violet would remind me to go and pay my respects to the oldest Kwan living in Shanghai at that time—Grandaunt # 9. We said prayers together, and then she would have a small gift for me—a silver dollar or something whimsical, like a fan. Grandaunt # 8, who was married into the Yung family, and had eleven children, often visited her son (my # 4 uncle) in Shanghai. Uncle # 4 was President of the Shanghai University. I went to their home on occasions, and also met Uncle # 9 who was home from the U.S. He had just earned his Doctorate in Botany. Actually, I had met Grandaunt # 8 at Ah Dong's house. She and her husband would come over to mediate her sister's (Grandauntie # 10 and Grandaunt # 11) arguments. Remember the ones with the "dead cat" issues.

When I wasn't daydreaming and could face up to the truth, I realized, that the problems I was having at this school were my own fault. You see, I held myself in a higher station from these drably dressed (army faded brown-grey) students—remnants of the old China. However, after many, many: 4:30 a.m. recitations of Dr. Sun Yat Sen's: "Last Message," my Mandarin improved, my attitude changed, I could communicate better and I even came to admire these students with their antiquated language (according to my standards). These young boys and girls stood straight and tall. Under harsh conditions, they applied themselves with earnest. Books were scarce: most classes were verbal only, and in the evenings, usually by oil lamp, they collaborated, and compiled written pages that could be used later for study. I met two very special girls at the school—Serenity and Beautiful Cloud. They made life bearable, and; even though, I tried very hard not to make friends (that I would have to eventually leave) they, without my noticing, broke through my guard, and stole my heart.

Serenity gave me much needed help with my school work: she taught me to open my mind to many sides of a discussion; she helped me to write essays objectively; she gently guided my thoughts (in Mandarin), when I wrote my mandatory diary. On Spring Break, she actually called me by my proper name ("Little Cantonese" disappeared after that), and invited me to her home. It was a long walk to Flower Torrene, and I was surprised at how out of shape I was, after a winter of inactivity. I had been so fit, when I first came to the school. When we arrived, the villagers were celebrating the Cherry Blossom Festival: they boated on the lake; they watched the melting snow form cascading waterfalls; they sat under the blossoming cherry trees. Here was beauty and peace. Serenity and I sat under a tree, and pinned blossoms in our hair, and wondered aloud what the future might hold for us.

Serenity's mother was imprisoned in her home (a soft cell). Her house was under constantly guarded surveillance, and she was of interest to the government. What government? I wondered—The Kuomintang? The Communist? The Japanese? She was a scholar, and her house had many books, and she wrote "papers" which were closely scrutinized. Serenity's father, who was also a scholar, and who was also being carefully watched, was away. He was with Mao Tse-tung (the Communist Party leader). Mao, of course, would be of interest to the Kuomintang and the Japanese, Serenity told me. The three of us spent many hours just talking. I surprised myself. I was interested in all the many topics that they discussed. No wonder Serenity did so well at school—she was educated at home.

It was Serenity and her mother who first made me aware of politics. They began to shape the nebulous cloud of thoughts I had about my country and about what was happening outside my own little world—they planted the seed. It wasn't until sometime later, in another school, far off from this place, that the seed would be watered and fertilized. Much later still, I would take its embryo to America—to study History. But, I have a long way to travel: ". . . a rough row to hoe, before I get there."

And, before I get ahead of myself, I very much want to tell you about Beautiful Cloud. She had decided, right from my first day at the school, that I was her charge. She recognized that I was a spoiled Cantonese-speaking misfit, who had little idea about practical matters. No matter how I tried to ignore her, she stuck to me like glue. She taught me: how to wash my clothes; how to mend a rip; how to pick rosemary, and soak it in the jug to use for washing my hair and bathing; how to fix my bed; how to make shoes—clean them; how to keep the charcoal burning . . . She willingly, and always with a smile, came to my aid. We laughed a lot, when I didn't understand something, and she had the patience of Job—she would say it over and over and over again, until I got it. When I woke up in the morning, after a particularly cold night, it would be her blanket that had given me extra cover.

Beautiful Cloud reminded me so much of my personal maids in Ah Dong's house—Little Snow and Lucky One. They did everything for me—no wonder I ended up a spoiled brat, unable to take care of myself. Ah Dong, who taught me to treat them with kindness and respect, had bought them from poor families. He paid for their night schooling (twice a week), and when they turned sixteen, he gave them a lump sum of money (according to their years of service), and provided tuition for them to take a trade. Lucky One became a tailor; Little Snow, staff at the share broker's market—she was extremely clever with numbers.

One day, Beautiful Cloud became critically ill. For the first time, I took Grandpa's medicine from my trunk. The school doctor was shocked that I had sulfanilamide, and asked to keep a portion. Because she was kept in isolation, in the infirmary, I don't know if they gave her Grandpa's medicine. I worried about her for three weeks, and then she came back to the dormitory. I had washed and aired her bedding (just as she had taught me), and had placed some wild flowers (the tiniest violets that I had ever seen) in an empty ink bottle, to welcome her back. Their small faces looked so cheerful. I was reminded of the framed cross-stitch sampler that hung in Auntie Violet's house, in Shanghai. It had tiny violets surrounding a quote from Shakespeare:

I know a bank where the wild thyme blows,
Where oxlips and the nodding violet grows,
Quite overcanopied with luscious woodbine,
With sweet musk-roses and with eglantine.

I had to climb up on a chair to copy the words. I put them on the front of one of my scribblers, and mother, being always practical, had packed it, because it still had many empty pages. I noticed the scribbler when I was getting Grandpa's medicine. I want to make two observations here. The first: When I had to climb up to see Auntie Violet's sampler, I realized, that Chinese people hang pictures and wall decorations very high up on the wall. In my dream, in Grandauntie # 10's room, I hung The Blue Boy and Matching Girl just above the elegant chair. They wouldn't have to look down on people entering the room. I wonder if they were calm and courageous like Grandauntie # 10, when the commando came. The second: Their Hawaiian Grandparents gave my mother and her sister their English flower names—Daisy and Violet. Because Chinese had trouble pronouncing V, Daisy became Dai Day (Big Daisy) and Violet became Sai Day (Little Daisy). Most relatives only know her as Sai Day, and they might not know who I've been talking about—this Auntie Violet. How I do get carried away. Beautiful cloud was pale and weak, and needed to be supported to walk, but she insisted, that she wanted to go home. Home was twenty five miles away by mountain path. I offered to walk with her. It was so strange: we would walk a ways, and then, be met by someone with a one-wheeled cart. We would be pushed 'till we came to a rest spot. The following day, someone else would meet us, and the same thing would be repeated. This went on for four days; then, she went on, and I turned back. In my previous experiences, going home from somewhere always seemed shorter, than going there in the first place. In this case, it was entirely the opposite—it seemed to take forever, to get back to the school.

I had a plan. I thought that if I walked very quickly, I could make it to the same resting spots where Beautiful Cloud and I had spent the nights. It wasn't the same travelling alone. Beautiful Cloud was weak, and she spoke little, and often fell asleep, in the cart, but she was there with me. When she was alert, she would call out, "Good morning Mr. Chickadee, did you have a good night?" "Good afternoon Mrs. Tufted Titmouse, how are your children?" She recognized many birds by their songs, and plants and shrubs that we saw by the wayside, by their berries or flowers. It was good for her to be out doors after being in bed all that time, and she enjoyed it. In the distance we saw waving blue flowers, and she told me it was a field of flax. I had noticed that people we passed or met wore a coarse linen fabric, but I had no idea that linen was made from flax. I missed her company, and where the path forked, I was nervous about going the wrong way. With hand gestures and few words, I attempted to ask people passing, if this was the way to the Temple School, and everyone nodded and pointed, but I didn't quite know if they understood me, or if they were just being helpful by nodding yes, yes, yes. It was getting dark, and I had no idea how far away my first planned stop was, so I was desperately gesturing to anyone I met: "to eat—to sleep," and each pointed me back in the direction that I had just come. I hadn't noticed any sort of "inn", so in complete confusion, I just hurried on. It wasn't long; however, and much to my relief, I did come to a place. I didn't recognize it, but decided I must try and stay here. It was O.K. and the keepers were nice enough, but it isn't very pleasant being all alone in a strange house. After I ate, I went to bed, determined to be up with the sun and on my way. They gave me a hearty breakfast and some cucumbers, tomatoes and plums to eat on my walk. They refused to take any money. I was beginning to think that maybe Beautiful Cloud's family was known along this way, and people were aware that I had accompanied her home.

I got an early start, and walked along at a good pace. Not stopping to take lunch, I ate as the mood struck me, and kept on going. In the early afternoon, I was surprised to come upon a rest spot where Beautiful Cloud and I had stayed. I recognized the well with a hand pump, and a big tree stump, with a huge jade plant sitting on it. Not knowing if I could reach another place to stay before dark, I decided to stay here. The keepers treated me like a long lost relative. They cut a Chinese sweet melon, and we sat outside at a small table, under a tree, in the shade. The melon was indeed very sweet, and so juicy that it dripped everywhere, so when we finished, we had to wash the stickiness off at the water pump. They let me help shell peas and scrub some carrots, and we took our evening meal together. They explained, the best they could, and I understood, that a cart would take me, the next day, to the next rest place, where Beautiful Cloud and I had stayed. What a relief! I didn't feel like I was alone, and I fell into bed and went fast asleep. I was taken care of, and the rest of my return trip went without incident, and no one would take any pay. The last cart let me off a few miles from the school, and knowing that safe haven was in easy reach, I sauntered along in a carefree fashion. Now that I knew for sure where the school was, I wasn't in any rush to return. Beautiful Cloud had pointed out some edible berries, so I climb the bank to try them: they were sweet and tasty, but a bit pulpy and dry in the mouth, so I sat on a rock, and not having to pace out my water any longer, I emptied my canteen, and swished out my mouth, which I assumed must be very blue from the berries. Suddenly a snake slithered past just a few inches from my shoes. Ever since my mother told me her story about snakes, they make me nervous, and I quickly returned to the path, and was on my way. I was watching a flock of swift-flying, fork-tailed birds swoop and dive and turn in unison, when I spotted someone coming towards me along the path. It was my "Friend Monk." I was so happy to see him, I could have hugged him to death, but that; of course, would have been most inappropriate. He had a bedroll tied like a sling over his back, and he carried a cloth sack, that I assumed contained some food. I hadn't known him to have left the temple before, so I was wondering if something had happened, and he was going to his village. He is very private, so I had to be discreet, and just simply asked where he was going. He told me, that he was worried that I might get lost, so he was given permission to come, to try to spot me. Obviously, he was prepared to be away overnight, if need be. How kind and caring! As a young boy, he had been sold to the temple by his family. They were very poor, and there were just too many mouths to feed. He considered himself lucky—he was not only fed, but he was given the opportunity to have an education, and he became very devoted to the teachings of the monks. We often sat on the school steps and talked. He was curious about Christianity and about our school and about the world outside his cloistered life.

He turned around, and then, we started to walk together. To make conversation, I told him about the snake that had frightened me, and to keep talking, I started telling him mother's snake story: My mother was born in Chang Wong. Her father (my Grandpa) had moved his medical practice there from Hong Kong, so he could be close to Nan King (the new capital of the Republic) to help Dr. Sun Yat Sen, when he became the first President. Grandpa bought a young houseboy from a poor family. Chang Wong, incase you don't know, I told "Friend Monk," is famous for its many and different kinds of snakes. Each household, at that time, kept a white snake as a pet. Because they were the alpha snake, they were used to protect the house from other snakes. It so happened, that a poisonous snake came into Grandpa's house, and before the white snake was aware of it, mother, who was a toddler, went to play with this invader. The young houseboy sized up the situation, and quickly threw a chair at the dangerous snake. It squeezed the chair to pieces. By this time, the white snake was alerted, came, and finished off the intruder. Grandpa recognized that the boy had intelligence, and; besides, he had probably saved mother's life, so Grandpa freed him from his house duties, and sent him to school. This boy, whose name is Wai, became a pharmacist. And, when I left home, he was still working for my Grandpa, I told "Friend Monk." He is treated like family, and he and Grandpa have been close and loyal friends over all those years. By the time I had finished the snake story, we had reached the school. I turned to "Friend Monk" and simply said, "Thank You." We went our separate ways, and I wondered if *we* had become close and loyal friends.

Now, I want to tell you about other special people that I met while at the Temple School. I have already told you, when I first came to the school, I missed the missionaries that I had been travelling with, and was often frustrated trying to communicate in Mandarin. When spring came, I escaped to the outdoors—I walked into the mountains behind the temple. I found silence, solitude and beauty. I really needed to think, uninterrupted, about home—about mother and my brothers, about Grandpa and Grandma, about Granduncle and Grandaunt # 12 and all the relatives that had flocked to them from Shanghai, and about Ah Dong. And, I wondered if Margeta had got safely home to England, and how she could possibly manage without her children. I had no idea how any of them were, of course, but it helped to spend some time thinking about them.

The school warned me not to get too close to the native people: they did not like to be disturbed. I don't recall seeing any men, but would often see women. The sunlight caught their silver jewelry, and I would spot them, heads piled high with bundles of firewood, cumbersomely, swathed in their long pleated skirts—Dàn Gān Qún (layer upon layer of material), waving their way on the pathways.

In the mountains there were many deep crevices that were bridged with narrow wooden planks. I had crossed these many times. The trick was to set your sights on the other side and not to look down. One day, I spotted a pile of upturned skirts on one of these crossings. A woman had fallen to her knees; couldn't get up. I didn't heed the warning to keep my distance, and using no words, I came slowly up behind her, and gently tried to raise her to her feet. Top heavy, we swayed back and forth, and backing up clumsily, we lost our balance, and she fell on top of me. Luckily, we had reached solid ground. Gesturing for me to follow, she crossed over the plank without further incident, and led me to her home. The place had been carved out of the mountain side (more or less like a cave), and was soon filled with women and children who came rushing to hear her story. I had seen many bee boxes on my visits in the mountains, so was not surprised, when the sweet cakes that they served, were made with honey. They treated me like a heroine. After that, when I spotted any of them, we would wave and stop and attempt a small conversation. One day a woman was tending her bee box, and she gestured me to come. She gave me a slice of honeycomb that was dripping. I had never tasted anything so sweet and delicious. After tasting the real thing (straight from the bee), honey that we get in a jar, will never be the same for me.

I could differentiate "my friends" from other minority groups that came down to the valley, twice a month, to "barter—trade." We students would go down to these markets. Mother's trunk came in handy: for maybe a needle, I could get a package of candy—honey-made, of course. And I could say, "Hello" to the mountain people.

Occasionally, older mountain children turned up at our school. They brought their opium guns, and they smelled funny, and their teeth were spotted brown. The teachers attempted to assimilate them, but language was a problem, and perhaps curiosity satisfied, they would be gone.

I had been back from going home with Beautiful Cloud for some time. It was getting on into late summer, when on my trips into the mountains, I first started noticing dogs with an arm or a leg or with some other human part. Then, I started seeing them—the walking Chinese soldiers. They were the farmers that I had seen on my travels, such a short time ago. They were ill-dressed, and wore straw slippers, or if these had come to nothing, they went barefoot, and their feet oozed with sores. Untrained and with rusted guns that were shared, they were headed to the "front" for combat. Food was scarce, and they were weak, and the foot disease wasn't contained, so they dropped like flies, and didn't have the strength to keep the feral dogs at bay. I had nightmares, and screamed out in my sleep—even though I had had practice in Hong Kong. I guess you never get used to such horrible conditions. I gave them Tiger Balm from mother's trunk.

It didn't take long before I realized that the situation was beyond my meager help. I reported what I had seen to the school authorities—the principal, Mr. Pang and Dr. Chiang. These two learned men, dressed "old fashioned" in the style of authority, gathered up their wisdom, and went to take a stroll. I couldn't help myself: they reminded me of the historical story of the "Three Kingdoms"—they went out to rule their kingdom. If it wasn't so serious a matter, it would have been comical. They were shocked by what they saw. And much to my great relief, they were shocked into action.

"All boys," they commanded, "Collect any thing that can be used; dig trenches, wherever possible around the school grounds." It was explained to us, that even though they would be in unmarked graves, these soldiers must be given a proper burial. One of the students wrote a beautiful a cappella song, and dedicated it to the soldiers.

"All girls," the teachers urged, "Collect used garments and rags; make shoes" The chapel (a small lean-to which had been built by the teacher-student-body) became a rest place for the soldiers and a hut, the first aid station. We were taught to wash the diseased feet with a dark-purple alum and to apply a mixture of Vaseline and Grandpa's sulfanilamide, and then, to wrap them in clean rags. We were instructed to gather certain plants, and to soften them on top of our bamboo heaters, and to wrap the plants around their feet, before they put on their new shoes, and trekked back out.

Not much, if any, school work got done. Everyone was busy with our war effort. And then, this routine too, came to a halt. An announcement came. The Japanese were only forty miles away. We must evacuate—immediately. We had to abandon the soldiers. In all likelihood, they joined the "walking dead."

The students left to go home to their families, and many offered to take me with them. It was difficult to know what to do. The teachers knew that "roads" had been built for war maneuvers. We might get down off the mountain and out to one of these, and hitch a ride on an army truck. Hopefully, we would go in the direction away from the advancing Japanese. Either of these two choices made taking mother's trunk impossible. The trunk was my ever-loosening hand-grip that I had on home. It wasn't possible for me to let go. Third choice: I went to talk to the monks. Perhaps they would shelter me here at the temple. I sought out "Friend Monk." He spoke to me very firmly, "You must leave! Before the Japanese come, the "bandits" will come. It will be a much crueler fate than facing the Japanese. They will capture you for life . . . The Japanese may only just kill you." "And," he continued without hesitation, "I am strong. I will help you get the trunk down to the road." He explained that I should stand by the side of the road where it takes a bend. There, all vehicles must slow down. He would hide in the ditch with my trunk, until one stopped.

"Friend Monk" was right: a truck stopped. It flew a British ensign and a small B.M.A. (British Military Aid) flag. I recognized them from Hong Kong. An English soldier, who wore many stars (high ranking I assumed), stepped out. I pulled out my passport, and hurriedly tried to explain that I was British protected personnel. I became painfully aware of just how bad my pigeon English had become. "And where might you be going?" "Chungking." I wasn't quite sure where this might be, but I knew it was the wartime capital, and thought it might be in the direction that I should be going. He signaled me to get in. "Friend Monk" popped up, and after much gesturing, he and the soldier loaded my trunk into the back of the truck, next to a cannon—the only other passenger. We took off. I couldn't recall if I had thanked my friend, or if I had said goodbye. I looked in the rearview mirror. He was waving mightily, with both arms in the air. That's the picture I will hold in my memory. Being such a callow thing, I hadn't even asked him his real name, and I had no idea if the temple might have an address. Grandpa and his friend Wai had taught me, that you have to nurture a friendship. How was I going to do that? I wouldn't even know how to get in touch. And "Friend Monk" had taught me such a very important life lesson—he had made me realize, that I judge people by what they wear. "Friend Monk's" heart and soul shone right through his coarse, simple, monk's robes. I shouldn't have held him at a distance, just because he was a monk. I should have embraced his humanity tightly to me, and I should have told him how much he was loved. I wondered if I would ever get a second chance.

Even though it was autumn, it was hot. Maybe from the exertion of getting the trunk down from the mountain and out to the road, or maybe because I hadn't eaten, or maybe from the emotional stress of indecision, I didn't feel well. I should have felt relief. I was on my way; hopefully, away from danger. I was shaky and feverish, and felt dazed. The soldier asked me who I knew in Chungking, and I mentioned Uncle S.S. (Granduncle # 6's son, the architect who came to Ah dong's house to discuss "The Book" with mother and Ah Dong). If any Kwan was in Chungking; most likely, it would be he. I wondered if I should tell him that Uncle S.S. was associated with Chiang Kai-shek. During war, would it be good or bad to be with the Nationalist Party leader? If it was a good thing, I could go on to tell him that Grandpa was a colleague and friend of Dr. Sun Yat Sen. I couldn't decide, so I told him that I had two brothers. I suspected that they might be somewhere near Chungking. When the Japanese attacked Peking, Paul was at school in Tientsin, and mother thought that the relatives would have taken him South. Kit had joined the National Air Force—he might be close to the wartime capital.

I have no idea how long we drove, or if there was any further conversation, or if I fell asleep, but; eventually, we stopped at a kind of bus station. He told me that I would be safe here, and that a bus left daily to Chungking. He unloaded my trunk; was gone. I sat down on the ground. A young boy came, and rummaged through my trunk, and took some things. I never moved; after that, I must have fainted.

When I woke up, I was in a house, in a bed. I couldn't figure out where I was. I recognized the people who were attending to me: they were from Hong Kong. Where was I? Then I knew who they were—they were Grandauntie # 10's "Little Flock" missionaries, the ones who I had made the deliveries to, on my bicycle. They had evacuated here—wherever here was? I knew that it was some place between the Temple and Chungking. They explained that they had been called to come to pick up this girl at the bus station. She was on the ground in poor condition. Apparently, when they saw that it was me—so skinny and barely recognizable, they couldn't believe their eyes. These kind people were good to me: they fed me; they sat by my bedside through my night terrors; they reminisced with me about the good times—before all this insanity started. We laughed about that bicycle. They knew how Kit, one Christmas, had relentlessly urged me to ask Grandpa for a bicycle. I couldn't ride; wasn't very athletic, and if the truth be known, I was more than a little fearful of such a contraption. Kit was persistent, "You could ride everywhere and explore. There's a great big world out there. You would be free. You could fly." He knew that Grandpa spoiled me. He was pouncing on an opportunity. It was the only way he was going to get a bicycle.

Something else happened that took my thoughts backward. It made me think of the starving boys in the orphanage—remember, I let them out at night to steal food. One day, there was a great raucous in the street. I was asked to come out to identify my goods and the boy that had stolen them from my trunk. He was on the wall, hanging from his hands; his feet were barely touching the ground. I pulled myself up tall, and with strength beyond my means, gave a very definitive, "No!"

Shortly after that, I left for Chungking. It was known, that the bus would have to make its way seventy-two times round and round the mountain, before we could reach our destination. It was nothing like the # 7 bus that took us to school in Kowloon Tong. For one thing, it didn't run on gasoline. There were two tanks on the roof that had to be constantly refilled with water, and wood had to be gathered to fuel some heater—maybe it ran on hot air?

The going was slow; my mind would wonder; I became quite weepy. Everything that had happened since that long-ago-December-morning was starting to take its toll on me. I thought about Cousin Gay falling off the school bus, and getting all blue and black, and wondered where he might be—in Hong Kong? In Shanghai with his mother (Auntie Violet)? I wept. I worried about the older ones: "And, all that I could think of, in the darkness and the cold, was that I was far from home, and my folks were growing old." Tears flowed. My four brothers—any thought of them would make me cry. I thought of Mungie's sweet potatoes; I cried.

Then, an air raid siren sounded: "Run!" "Run!" "Run!" We ran; hid wherever possible. The bus was quickly covered with branches. The mosquitoes (Japanese war planes) flew low, and machine gunned everything in their sights.

If the Japanese were dropping incendiary bombs ("burning bombs", "burning eggs"), and if we were unfortunate to be too close, we would see a village swiped out in a matter of minutes—nothing left to rescue. I *see* the dying Chinese soldiers, horrifically, in my dreams, but what I *hear* is far worse—yelling for help; screaming in agony; gasping for life, or maybe for death; silencing of a village—the loudest sound of all. I wake up in a sweat with my hands covering my ears.

I was numbed by it all. I never shed a tear. Mother's voice came to me, "If you can't shed a tear, when you see people suffering; then, you have lost all reason to live." I was a young girl, all alone in a world that had gone mad, frightened beyond words; maybe, I had no reason . . . I forced myself to imagine that some good would rise out of these burned out villages: "Up from ancient ashes sprung, the mighty pine, / their crowns, loftier in the sky."

I had no idea if the bus had gone round and round the mountain seventy-two times. Finally, I realized it was still: didn't have any notion of going on. People got off; I got off. No one announced that this was Chungking; no sign declared it. My trunk was unloaded, and I stood there beside it. No thoughts came about what I should do. I just stood. Eventually, a foreigner came up, and asked to see my passport. I had few words left in me; especially, no English would come out. Somehow, he made me understand that I should go with him—I obeyed.

I was taken to a big black and white house: a butler opened the door, and I was taken care of by the staff. After a few days of baths with delicious smelling sandalwood soap, hot soups and lots of sleep, I was well enough to appreciate that I had been brought to a very beautiful place. The floors were well polished, were scattered with expensive rugs, and the living room had a large picture window. The view of the Chungking Valley was overwhelmingly majestic. There was also, a grand piano. I was in the home of the British Counsellor General. Mr. Shepherd was most gentle and very kind. He told me to make myself at home; to play the piano if I wished. He said that he knew my Uncle S.S. Kwan, and, that he could locate him for me. When I heard my uncle's name, I wept. This time, they were tears of joy.

The day came, and Uncle S.S. sent his office staff to pick me up. The main town of Chungking is on the North Shore of the Yangtze River. The South Shore is mountainous, very scenic, and the "established" have homes here. Chiang Kai shek had a place here, in an area called the Wong Mountain. Uncle S.S. built his home (The Clearwater—named after a creek that ran by it) on the South Shore. The Clearwater was simple but artistic. It was modeled in the style of the local farmer's houses—one bedroom, one very large sitting-dining-room. The cooking was done in a separate hut. Uncle S.S. was most proud of the bricks that were used in the construction—handmade from straw and the indigenous yellow clay.

That evening, when I arrived at this house, I was shocked to find the large room filled with people on the floor in sleeping bags. They were all Kwans: all refugees in need of a place to stay. In the morning, they disappeared to work or to school. To my great delight, I found Paul and Sylvia (his new bride) here with Uncle S.S. Later, when Paul found work, they moved into their own one-room apartment. And, to my further joy, they told me that Kit was here at the air base, down by the river. He had recently returned from Air Force Officer's training in the U.S. He was proudly flying a B 38. We talked and talked into the night—reminisced. We laughed, when we recalled how Kit could make "my" bicycle "fly." We all knew that one day he would be a pilot. Now, he was.

They were anxious to tell me the funny story about Kit's first visit here to Uncle S.S.'s house: The Yangtze River, after thousands of years of corrosion, now ran in a gorge many hundreds of feet down. After leaving the air base, Kit would have to walk up hundreds of steps to the South Shore, and then, would take the local transportation to Uncle S.S.'s house. The local transportation was two bamboo sticks held together in the middle by a woven rope seat. Two strong skillful men would carry their passenger. They would make necessary adjustments, according to the twist and tilt of the pathway, so the rider wouldn't tumble out. I need to tell you that Kit was very tall and extremely athletic. At school, he excelled in pole vaulting and running, and had won many metals. He had just finished military training, so was very fit. He was eager to show off his prowess, and instead of riding, he arrived at Uncle S.S.'s house carrying the sedan man.

I didn't see Paul and Kit very often. Paul was busy with his work; Kit was away many times on flying missions; I had to go to school. However, I remember; so well, those happy times together in Chungking. Maybe because happiness was such a scarcity, I locked those few happy times away—safely, in my memory.

Uncle S.S. enrolled me in Nankai School. It had a history of being progressive, and was the Alma Mater of some very successful people. 5th Uncle (S.Y.), another son of Granduncle # 6—the one that went to Tientsin and became physician to the Dowager—just incase you've forgotten, and his friend Chou En-lai, were graduates. I've already told you that Serenity and her mother planted the seed in me. The students in Nankai were actively involved in current affairs. They were the ones that fertilized and watered that seed, and I became interested in my country and what was going on. Each student had to declare whether they were a Nationalist or a Communist, and had to carry a card. Both 5th Uncle and Chou En-lai followed Mao Tse-tung. Chou En-lai would become a stalwart supporter, a moderating force in the Communist Party. He was respected by most Chinese people (of all stripes, and was popular with western leaders), and when he died was given a hero's funeral—a "poet's memorial". But, I digress. What I meant to say, was that I was influenced by my uncle and his friend, and was; also, bombarded by the Communist Party on campus. I learnt that Maoism was a form of Marxism—Leninism. I already knew, from Grandpa, about the Nationalists. I've told you many times already that his colleague and family friend, Dr. Sun Yat-Sen, was the Founding Father of the First Republic. Later, four groups that formed that Republic, amalgamated, and named this new party the Kuomintang—the Nationalist Party. Chiang Kai-shek became the leader.

It was during my time at Nankai, that the United States officially got involved in our war: the "Marshall" gave aid to both parties. It was 5th Uncle and Chou En-lai that accepted the Communist's share.

At school, everything wasn't all current affairs and politics. I was determined to graduate. I had lost so much time over the last three years. I had to settle down to the books—luckily, Nankai was blessed with many.

However, when I'm thinking of Dr. Sun Yat Sen, I want to tell you something that Grandpa told us, at one of those family gatherings (I think it was a one-month-party for Nancy—Honkie and Margeta's daughter). It seems like a life time ago. Anyway, Grandpa told us that when Sun was ill, he went to visit him. The guards at the gates to his house were not impressed by this scruffy looking man in a wrinkled western suit, and they were not about to let him pass. Grandpa told them, to tell Sun, that Kwan was here. Sun, in his bed clothes, came down to meet him, and was very pleased that he had come, and ushered him into his private quarters. The household, not to mention the guards, were shocked. The two old friends didn't exchange formalities. The plaque on Sun's desk said everything of the past that needed to be said:

> Bliss was it in that dawn to be alive,
> But to be young was very Heaven!
> (Wordsworth)

Sun had a very serious matter on his mind. He entrusted a large sum of his private money to Grandpa. It was to be used as scholarships for students who had lost their means of support during the revolution, and could not afford an education. Grandpa was to work out the details. I had wondered at the time, but didn't ask, if it went to their old alma mater—Diocesan Home and Orphanage (DHO) which was now called Diocesan School Orphanage (DSO). Dr. Sun Yat Sen died at the young age of 55 on March 12th, 1925.

I had just started a serious attack into my studies, when I heard on the radio an announcement by Generalissimo Chiang Kai-shek. The war was officially over. PEACE was declared. It was August 15, 1945. *He praised the Chinese for their heroic struggle, but also gave credit to the allies.*

In cities from Shanghai to Chungking and in rural areas almost everywhere, men, women and children—a few hundred million—poured out of their houses yelling and cheering. The Japanese soldiers remained in their barracks in a daze. Millions upon millions of fire crackers crackled through the night and long into the next day. It was arguably the biggest celebration in human chronicles and a great moment in Chinese history. The Americans and the atom bomb had defeated the Japanese, but this fact did not distract from the sense of a great Chinese victory. After all, the Chinese felt that they had done their part all those years, taking out more than a million Japanese soldiers and as many as a thousand enemy war planes. I was so proud that my brother had done his part.

Some five hundred miles to the north of Chungking, in Mao Tse-tung's headquarters in the town of Yan'an, the celebration of V-J Day was muted. The Chinese people viewed the triumph as Chiang Kai-shek's victory. Neither Chiang nor Mao was celebrating. The Nationalists and the Communists had been fighting off and on for over twenty years to see which party and leader would guide China toward fulfilling its dream—a great nation restored. The two parties had formed a united front against the Japanese. That war was over. "Peace" had been declared. Now, Civil War could begin.(The images of the people's reaction to the war's end came from the website:Sino-Japanese war).

"Not another war!" "Not more fighting!" How was I ever going to get my high school diploma?

I remember so well the day I ran into Kit on the steps. He was coming down from the North Shore on his way to the airbase. The National Air Force was busy developing and testing aircraft, and Kit hadn't yet been dismissed from duty. I happened to be going up, and we stopped to talk.

He stood so straight and tall: so handsome in his uniform. He emptied his pockets, and gave me all the money he had. "Why?" I questioned him. I think he knew that mother's "diamond money" was coming to an end. I had recently cashed the last commodity certificate that Mrs. Lien had exchanged from Japanese military money—a million years ago, in that small port in Fukien. I had been protecting this last certificate. It had been with me for a long time, through so many things, and when I finally let it go, I felt mother slipping away from me. "Keep it," Kit said, and off he went, jauntily down the steps—two at a time. It reminded me of when we were at home, Kit would dash up the stairs to Ah Dong's study, and Ah Dong would make him go down again, and approach his study with dignity. Kit was always in a hurry. He had:

Places to go, things to do, before it got dark. (Robert Frost)

I watched him until he went out of sight—was gone. How was I to know? It wasn't mother who was slipping away. Those were Kit's last words—I would never see him again.

I was at school when it happened. Kit's Group Commander came to see me. He had Kit's uniform over one arm, and carried his other belongings: a box with his medals; a sealed brown envelope which contained among other things, an unfinished letter to mother. It took me sometime to take in what was happening. Later, when I remembered that the commander cried, I felt that he cared, and I was some how comforted. Kit died at the young age of 22 on December 8th, 1945.

Kit was dead; Paul left; Uncle S.S. had to go to Nanking; I was left alone. I was numb from emotional exhaustion—I just wanted to go home. Before he left, Uncle S.S. told me that I must stay in Chungking; wait for him to return. He would bring an airline ticket, so I could leave.

On my own, I went to visit my old school from Shanghai. I knew they had evacuated here to Chungking during the war. The school was buzzing with activity. Everyone was busy packing up to leave—they were going back to Shanghai. The principal recognized me, and told me, that they had chartered a "White Wood Boat." There was a seat available; the cost was such and such. I reserved the seat, and went back to Uncle S.S.'s house. How could I find that kind of money? At the house there was an elderly woman (the cook) and a young boy whose name was Little Pig. We called him "The Butler." I checked the contents in my trunk: a few woolen sweaters; a warm silk jacket; other items that I wouldn't need anymore. I asked "The Butler" if he would go to the street, and sell these things. We would split half and half. "And sell the trunk," I told him. "It probably has some value these days with everybody on the move." He sold everything. My share was three thousand dollars—more money than I had left Hong Kong with. I could buy my ticket on the "White Wood Boat" to Nanking, my fare, by train, to Shanghai and pay my fees for school, once it got set up again. The principal thought I probably had a half year more of studies before I could graduate.

The day before I was to meet down by the river to depart, Uncle S.S. came home. He was excited, and handed me the airline ticket. I had some explaining to do. I said that I had found an opportunity, and had seized it. I described the "White Wood Boat": how it would be just like the ocean liner (with the three blue chimneys) that mother had taken us on. He gently took me to the window, and told me to look down. The river was crowded, on both sides, with many boats (oversized sam pans), waiting to take people to Nanking. He told me about the place on the Yangtze called the Ghost Gate—Hell's Gate—the Gate of the Devil. There is an up-cropping in the middle of the channel: this divides it into two narrow passage ways, and causes the water to swirl in strong currents. Many boats, he explained, capsize here, and are sucked down by the current. He spoke to me very seriously, "I have your mother to answer to: she has lost your father: she has recently lost Kit." We stood there looking down at the river. Part of the airbase was visible. I think he was letting what he had said sink in. Finally, he started to speak again, "I can see that you are just like your mother. You saw an opportunity, and you took action. All too many people, in uncertain times, are paralyzed by hesitation. Here are two hundred dollars, buy three life jackets. You can swim; perhaps, with these, you will survive." This wonderful uncle had worked with young people. He wasn't one to squash their initiatives. He had discovered and supported Mr. Yang, the well known athlete who won Silver for China in the Austrian Olympic Games.

The boat, indeed, was no ocean liner. With sails and five oarsmen on each side to propel it, and a rudder to steer it by, it was, just as Uncle had said, an over-sized sam pan. We passengers: the principal; five teachers; a pregnant guest and me, boarded and found it quite adequate. The boat was ingeniously designed. Every square inch was utilized—the beds were stacked bunks on both sides of the cabin.

The country was at war. Mao was using guerilla tactics against Chiang. This war; however, was different than the one we had just suffered through. Chinese were fighting Chinese. Brother might be fighting brother. I don't know what was happening in other parts, but where we travelled, there was an unwritten rule: fighting took place from 5 p.m. to 5 a.m.—in the day time, people just went about their daily living. This rule necessitated a strict schedule for our movement. The boat started out at 5 a.m. and was in port by 5 p.m. In this slow manner we stopped in, at least, fifty small villages as we went down river. The villages were separated by mountains and many streams, and were connected by footpaths. The one-seat sedans were very prevalent. If the boat came to port early, we would climb the steps up to the village to have a look around, to meet the elder (the wise old man), and if time allowed, to have dinner. Food in the villages was cheap and fresh—mostly garden vegetables, newly caught fish, eggs and rice. I can still taste those meals—they were simple and delicious.

Sure enough, we came to Hell's Gate. Our boat hit something, the rudder left. We started turning round and round—faster and faster. There was great panic, and the oarsmen jumped into the water—they knew what was coming. Everyone was being tossed about, and they were grabbing for anything to hang on. I crawled on my hands and knees; hopelessly, trying to get to the life jackets. There was a thunderous clap, the sail swung, snapped, and "dues ex machina", we shot forward—were left in calmer waters near the shore.

I want to tell you something that happened while we waited for the boat to be repaired. We were in a village tea house. The weather was cold, and they were serving Hot Rice Wine (you could smell the fermented rice) with a poached egg on top—it was delicious. We were enjoying this treat, when in walked a group of Japanese soldiers, still in uniform, the red suns still on their sleeves. They walked straight to the counter, and put four or five watches down. The owner served them the Hot Rice Wine. I was furious. I still had nightmares over the Chinese soldiers, and I could still hear the screams of agony in those burning villages, and the brown stain on the wall behind the counter was probably Chinese blood, and the watches were probably taken from Chinese prisoners, and my brother was dead. I went berserk. I ran to the owner and shouted, "How could you?" "How could you?" I was shaking and crying and yelling, and he gently guided me to sit down. When I was finished yelling, he said, "For many years we have waited for this war to be over. Our country has declared peace with these people. Everyone must make an effort to make it happen. These men are waiting for their government to send them home." Here, in this remote village, high above the Yangtze River, this humble tea house owner taught me a most valuable lesson about forgiveness—he deserved the Nobel Peace Prize.

After fifty two days we reached Nanking. I went straight to search for Uncle S.S.—he had gone to Shanghai. So I boarded the train to follow him. The strangest thing happened. When my train was approaching Shanghai station, it slowed down. On the tracks beside me was a slow-moving departing train. I saw a man waving violently. Uncle S.S. had spotted me looking out at the window, and he was desperately trying to get my attention. I waved. It was our destiny: we were always leaving each other. I knew, however, that he would be overjoyed. He had seen me arriving safely in Shanghai—there would be "lots of Kwans in sight" to take care of me. What good news he had to send to mother. While waiting to hear from the school, I had a few days stay with Auntie Violet's family. I had worried about Cousin Gay, so was very happy to find him safely at home.

The United Christian High School (Shanghai and Soochow amalgamated) set up on Soochow campus. The buildings had suffered a lot of damage. Local workers, the teachers and the students (as they returned) all pitched in to make the school functional. Eventually, classes started. I graduated. I received my High School Diploma—finally. I was asked, over and over, how I felt. I had just studied poetry. I felt like Robert Louis Stevenson's: "much exposed cow." I had been: "blown by all the winds that pass / and wet with all the showers."

Paul was also in Shanghai. He bought us tickets: Sylvia and I went home to Hong Kong—to mother.

Hong Kong was not the Hong Kong that I had left. Not the place. Not the people. War had left the place run down—shabby. Grandpa was not there. Ah Dong was very frail. Mother was much older. I gave her Kit's uniform, his other belongings and the envelope with the unfinished letter. She cradled them to her heart. An eternity passed: silence held the tender sadness. When she could speak, she didn't speak of Kit. She told me letters had arrived: I could go to university in the U.S.; I had received two scholarships. We talked about it for awhile, but mostly, we talked about the good things that had happened over the five years we had been apart. She came to realize, that I couldn't leave—not just yet. So, I had time just to be home.

Uncle Honkie also came back to Hong Kong. I was surprised to see David and Nancy. They were babies when I last saw them. Now, they were in school. Later, he brought his mother (Grandaunt # 13) back to live with him. It was wonderful to see them making up for lost years. I remember him dancing his father up the stairs. Now, he would swoop up his mother in his arms, and carry her aloft to her room. I haven't had a chance to tell you, and I would definitely be amiss if I don't. Mother told me, on many occasions, just how wonderful a mother Grandaunt # 13 was to her and her little sister. Mother said that she didn't know how she and Violet would have managed, after their mother died, if it hadn't have been for Grandaunt # 13. Grandaunt # 13 was very affectionate—she would hug and kiss the little girls, and with big English mugs of cacao, they would climb up on her bed for story time. She kept a steamer trunk full of dresses and purses, and she would help them dress-up, and they would pretend to travel all over the world. They went by ocean liner to England or Australia or even to the Americas. If it was hot, they would go to Hawaii, out in the shade, next to the maid's quarters, and have lemonade. When mother came back to her childhood home, after living in Kuala Lumpur, she looked for that steamer trunk, but it was gone.

Remember, I told you that in 1930 when we first went to Ah Dong's house, Grandaunt #11 (the one that gave me the beautiful dress) and her son Uncle Y went to Tientsin to live with Granduncle and Grandaunt # 14. Uncle Y became a surgeon, and married # 14's daughter—Amy. She's the beautiful young lady, in the picture, on the desk, in the living room, at Ah Dong's house. Now, Granduncle # 14, Grandaunt # 11 and Uncle Y have all passed away. Ah Dong urged Grandaunt # 14 and Amy to come home. I was able to meet their boat, and was shocked when I met Amy. I was expecting a beautiful lady. Her face was scarred beyond recognition. This is her story: She was a dentist—a graduate from Columbia University. She had her practice in Tientsin. One night she went to her laboratory to work on dentures for her father. Because it was late, she locked the door. Somehow, she set the place on fire, and before anyone could get to her, she was severely burned. Her husband used his own skin in an attempt to reconstruct her face, but; even so, she was left badly deformed.

Ah Dong had a small bungalow across from the Garden Triangle, and he had it fixed up for them. It was nothing compared to their mansion in Tientsin, but they seemed happy in that little house. Amy's picture; however, stayed undisturbed with Ah Dong.

Also, when I had this time to myself, I went to Canton to visit Grandaunt # 8's daughter (# 2)—Aunt Edith Yung. She and my mother were close and dear cousins. She had attended Wellesley College, which was rare for a Chinese of her time. I enjoyed my ten day visit with her. She was gracious and intelligent, and we had wonderful conversations, that I found helpful in anticipation of my trip to university in the States. Shortly after my visit, it happened. She was on a mission to raise funds for war orphans, when her ship hit a mine, and she was killed.

It didn't seem like I was home very long when genetics again took over my mother. We were talking, once more, about my education. When I said goodbye to Ah Dong, he could only nod his head in approval, and whispered, "Take care of your mother." I didn't have the opportunity to pay my respects to him until years later. I had taken that "embryo" to the states; had graduated with a degree in History; had married; had moved to Singapore to live, and then, one day I went back to Hong Kong. I needed to say a proper goodbye to my dear Ah Dong. Auntie Violet's husband took me to the cemetery. I had some small bouquets to leave. First, we stopped at the Great Grandparents orange-brown marble marker. All those years ago, when I had been polishing it, I had thought that in life, death was a given—it all depended on when someone might carve the numbers into the stone. I had been wrong—the death numbers hadn't been added, but I knew that most of the Grand Uncles and Aunts were now dead. I assumed that after the war, the stone carvers had a long list of catching up to do, or the person who took care of these things was among the ones with the missing numbers. I thought of the borrowed flowers that I had placed on graves, so that the dead wouldn't feel forgotten. I thought of the grave somewhere in Chungking and the young man, twenty-two-years of age, who had sacrificed his life. At that moment, a butterfly came, and landed on my flowers, and a warm feeling of peace washed through me—Kit knew that he wasn't forgotten, and never would be. When we came to Ah Dong's grave, it was a mass of white orchids. What a glorious sight—such a fitting tribute. Closure.

EPILOGUE

I relived it all: the happy; the sad; the horrific. I re-felt all the emotions: I laughed; I cried. The night mares returned, and I shook with terror. I thought, endlessly, about all those places and all those people. I would sit, and think about say, for instance—Beautiful Cloud, and an hour would be gone. It's a miracle that I got any words to paper. Then, at times, the words flowed on the tears, and ran quickly across the page—seeking permanence. It makes me ponder my life. Not the why-me-s? But the what-if-s! What if, I hadn't been born at that time? In that place? But especially, what if, I hadn't been born into the Kwan family?

I know that there are thousands of Kwans out there, and that many of you travel. If ever you find yourself at Ah Dong's church in Hong Kong, on the Star Ferry, on Waterloo Road in Kowloon Tong (touch the plaques at # 101,107,115—look across the street, on the hill, to Mary Noll Convent—turn, and look up to Lions Mountain—imagine the planes coming through), at D.B.S., at the Alice Hospital/ University of Hong Kong, at the Christian cemetery (look for the names), at the Ming Temple (I'm sure it must still be there. Take a walk in the mountains to see if the people still live in their cave-like houses; if they still keep bees), by Nankai School, on the South Shore in Chungking (look for my uncle's house—yellow bricks, for Chiang Kai shek's place—there must be a plaque), on the steps down to the Yangtze River in Chungking (remember Kit, let him represent all the young boys who gave their lives for your country), or at any of the other places that I've mentioned, stop and pause awhile, you are standing on your history—on Kwan history. I believe that it's a special place.

POSTSCRIPT

1. I must mention the relatives that took special care of me during my university days in the U.S. Grandaunt # 8's son, Uncle #6 and Aunt #6. Phoebe Yap (Aunt #6 was her mother's sister) and I spent many of our school holidays with them. They made sure that we didn't miss the excitement of New York. They treated us to Radio City, Carnegie Hall, 5th Avenue Christmas window displays, and the New Year Apple Drop. Grandaunt # 8's son, Dr. Winston Yung, moved to Singapore to be the director of the South East Asia branch of the World Health Organization. Grandaunt # 8 lived with this son, and I got to know her well at that time. Winston's son Richard (my cousin) and his family (in Singapore) became very close, and his children and grandchildren are still very dear to me.

2. I met 9th Uncle Yung when I was in school in Shanghai. He had just returned from the U.S. He later became involved with the Ling Nam University, and still later founded the Chinese University in Hong Kong. I visited 4th Uncle Yung's home in Shanghai. I came to know his sons and their wives—Kenneth and Esther, Wally and Irene. They live in Canada, and I've met their children—Sylvia, Edith, Kenneth and Cynthia and grandchildren—Zacharey, Hailey, Anaia, Kienna, Kaezen, Trevor and Erin on my trips there.

3. When I was in Shanghai, I went to visit Grandaunt # 9. Even though her children, grandchildren and great grandchildren are scattered all over South East Asia, I've come to know them very well. In Shanghai—4th Aunt, 5th Uncle. In Hong Kong—3rd Aunt. In Singapore—2nd uncle. In Thailand—1st Aunt and daughter May and children.

4. As for Granduncle # 6's line: You know already that I knew Uncle S.S. and Uncle S.K. and his son Jack in Chungking. Uncle # 3, cousins Jean and Steven and Uncle #6 and son Kenneth, I met in San Francisco. Actually, Cousin Kenneth seemed to turn up every where—Shanghai, Hong Kong (at # 107 Waterloo Road) and in many places in the U.S. Because I haven't mentioned it before, and because Mother often

spoke of it endearingly, I want to mention that Mother went to Peking in 1919 to visit her ailing Uncle # 6. She often referred to it as the trip that she was most happy that she had made.

5. After the war, the Japanese commando invited Mungie and Mother to visit him in Japan.

6. Paul and Sylvia eventually went to live in Happy Valley in Hong Kong. They have two sons—James and Tommy. They moved to Vancouver, Canada in the 1960s. James and Judy have two sons—Jeffrey and Christopher. Tommy and Julia have a son—Kameron. Paul and Sylvia have passed away, but the rest still live in Vancouver.

7. Mungie trained in radiology at Queen Mary Hospital in Hong Kong and in London, England. He married Christine, and they have two children—Jeffrey and Carol. They moved to New York in the 1960s. Carol is married to Brett and they have two sons—Sebastian and Kai. They live in Los Angeles. Mungie, Christine and Jeffrey still live in New York.

8. Ching followed in his Grandfather's and Granduncles' footsteps and went to what became Diocesan Boys' School (DBS). After graduation he went to Vancouver for University. He is married to Marlene and they have two children—Danny and Diana. Danny and Evelyne have three sons—Joshua, Jacob and Jérémie. They live on Vancouver Island. Diana and Joe have three children—Emma, Bayley and Carter. They live in Maple Ridge (just outside of Vancouver).

9. I married K.T. Quek, and after graduation we went to Singapore to live. K.T. had a daughter from his first marriage—Ah Ling, and we had three children together—Timmy, Sammy and Angela. K.T. has passed away. Timmy and Kimberly have a daughter Natalie. Timmy is now married to Susan. They all live in Seattle, Washington. Sammy and Alice and their son Andrew live in New Jersey. Angela and Mike live on a many-acre-farm on Vancouver Island. They designed and built a fabulous barn for their horses and a fantastic house on a lake. My childhood dream came true. When I visit on British Columbia's coast, I get to see Emily Carr's magnificent trees.

10. Cousin Gay married Pansy and they have two sons—Peter and Daniel. In the late 60s they moved to Ontario. The boys are both married and have children. Cousin Gay's brothers are scattered throughout Canada and the U.S.—Hawaii, New York, and California.

11. Uncle Honkie's daughter, Nancy Kwan, became famous when she played Suzy in the movie: "The World of Suzy Wong" (1960). She now lives in Los Angeles.

12. When Paul had a place in Hong Kong, Mother and her most faithful servant (King King) went to stay with him. She simply handed the key to #115 Waterloo Road to Honkie. This house was her childhood home. This house is where she raised her children. This house is where she nursed Grandauntie # 10 and Ah Dong during their last days. This house was where she faced all the war crises. This house was where she had said goodbye to Kit, and where the news of his death was received.

Honkie told her that she was more a part of the house than he was. She said, "Come what may." And nothing came of it. It was the same thing, when she finally, after the war, had time to check on the legalities of Father's estate—nothing came of it.

She went to work as a matron at the Y.W.C.A. Hostel. She lived-in at the Y, so King King went to live with her own brother. In 1966 Mother went to Vancouver. She spent her time between New York and Vancouver in her sons' homes. Then, for the first time in her life, at the age of 78, she moved into a place of her own. She loved it, and held court for many of her friends visiting from Hong Kong, and held Bible study groups there. Auntie Emily Yap (the neighbour from Kuala Lumpur days and life long friend) was a frequent visitor, as was, Auntie #11 (Grandaunt # 8's daughter). Auntie # 11 lived in Vancouver with her daughter Jeannie, Frank and their two sons. The most special friend who came to visit was King King. All the Vancouver relatives, who had heard so much about this faithful lady, were pleased to meet her, at last. She stayed a month, and then was on her way to visit her sisters in the U.S. She had saved her money and educated these sisters, who now wanted her to stay with them and have an easy life. She couldn't handle a life of leisure, so instead, decided to go back to Hong Kong to live with her brother. Mother shopped, cooked and entertained without any help, and relished the independence of it all. She took herself, by Sea Bus, across Burrard Inlet, to China Town, for church. It reminded her of going over to

Hong Kong side by ferry to Ah Dong's church. The last task that she wanted to complete was to translate "Revelations" into Chinese for her church group. Isn't it interesting? Her grandfather had helped translate the 1st Chinese Bible in 1867, and now, here she was, in the 1980s, doing the same thing. When she was finished, she cooked, and had the family members over for dinner to celebrate. She passed away that night in her sleep—1985-90 years of age, in the Chinese way of counting.

13. The Kwan Family Book of Records that was compiled by Granduncle # 6, Granduncle # 13, Kwan Wai-Hing (7-3) (mother), and Kwan S.S. (6-1) is in the library at the University of California at Berkley. It was last edited in 1937 and was then named the Kwan Genealogy Record.

14. It is interesting to note that on March 29th, 1974, the First Emperor's necropolis was found. 8,000 terracotta warriors, many chariots and numerous horses were unearthed. Xi'an has now become a very popular tourist destination. And, there are many pomegranate trees surrounding the area. Kit would have been pleased to know that the Emperor didn't have his real army buried alive with him.

15. The description of the Chinese people's reaction to the announcement that the war was over came from the website: Sino-Japanese War.

16. In 2011 a statue of Dr. Sun Yat Sen was erected in the courtyard at D.B.S.. It may commemorate him as a student (circa 1883); however, I choose to believe it stands for the spirit of the man who believed that a good education is the entitlement of all, and that lack of financial means should not be a barrier. This is the same unwritten spirit that is so deeply embedded in the Kwan Family Motto.

ABOUT THE AUTHOR

Marlene Cheng

Marlene took on this project; not only, because she has been fascinated with Chinese history and culture ever since her university days, when she took a course in Asian Studies, but; mainly, to help Man Sheung fulfill her family reunion obligations. She has met, and knows many of the family members mentioned in the story.

Marlene found Man Sheung's critique of the finished project interesting. True to her "artsy" thinking, she compares it to a salad:

"I provided the main ingredients--lettuce, vegetables and a few tomatoes. You added the "bits and pieces" and "this and that" of special ingredients, gleaned from Mother and other family members that went to Canada. But, the salad dressing, that gives it the unique taste, is in the telling. It has a balance of Western and Chinese flavours--so in keeping with our family, all the way back to Great Grandmother Kwan."

Marlene is married to Man Sheung's youngest brother, Ching (Richmond). They live in West Vancouver, B.C.

MY FAMILY ALBUM

故事圍繞孫中山與革命同志〝四大寇〞的事績，革命之路隨即展開！

圖：「四大寇」孫中山、尤列、陳少白、楊鶴齡與關景良（後站者）
於香港西醫書院合照，1888年。

SUN YAT SEN (2nd FROM LEFT) AND HIS GROUP OF 4 AT MEDICAL SCHOOL (1888). LATER, GRANDPA KWAN #7, (STANDING) MOVED HIS MEDICAL PRACTICE TO CHANG WONG (WHERE MOTHER WAS BORN), CLOSE TO NAN KING, TO HELP SUN WHEN HE BECAME PROVISIONAL PRESIDENT OF THE FIRST REPUBLIC OF CHINA.

The original photo is in the medical school archives. This photo was scanned from a poster for a play—Rising Sun—in Hong Kong, 2010.

GRANDMA KWAN

THIS IS GRANDPA KWAN'S FIRST WIFE. SHE WAS FROM HAWAII. HER FATHER, A PLANTATION OWNER, SUPPORTED SUN YAT SEN'S REVOLUTION. SUN INTRODUCED HER TO GRANDPA. SHE WAS PART HAWAIIAN, PART CAUCASIAN AND PART CHINESE. NO WONDER SHE WAS SO BEAUTIFUL. MOTHER WAS THEIR THIRD CHILD. AFTER THE SEVENTH CHILD, SHE DIED. THAT'S WHEN MOTHER AND AUNTIE VIOLET WENT TO LIVE AT #115 WATERLOO ROAD, KOWLOON TONG WITH GRANDUNCLE #13 (AH DONG) AND GRANDAUNT #13.

GRANDMA KWAN (2ND WIFE) AND GRANDPA KWAN. THEY HAD NINE CHILDREN. HER ANCESTORS WERE KAT PEOPLE (BOAT PEOPLE) WHO ENDED UP IN HAWAII—SO SHE, LIKE HIS FIRST WIFE, IS PART HAWAIIAN.

MY FATHER—YUN TIN CHENG—HE DIED FEB. 25, 1941 BEFORE THE JAPANESE INVASION DEC. 1941. HE'S ON THE RIGHT.

MY MOTHER—DAISY WAI HING KWAN

GRANDUNCLE # 13—AH DONG IN HIS BELOVED GARDEN.

AH DONG'S HOUSE WHERE WE LIVED—#115 WATERLOO ROAD, KOWLOON TONG.

MOTHER AND PAUL

MOTHER, ME AND MUNGIE

KIT

COUSIN GAY

COUSIN ELEANOR'S
MOTHER AND CHING.

MARGETA (HONKIE'S WIFE) AND HER SON DAVID. HER
DAUGHTER NANCY WAS A BABY. AFTER THIS PICTURE, I
DIDN'T SEE THEM AGAIN UNTIL AFTER THE WAR—THEY
WERE SCHOOL CHILDREN.

GRANDMA KWAN AND SOME OF HER CHILDREN. HER DAUGHTER—1ST ON THE LEFT, NEXT TO HER #16—HE WAS A BOY SCOUT IN THE STORY, NEXT TO HIM IS S.C., AND IN FRONT OF HIM IS S. YEE WHO HAD HIS 100TH BIRTHDAY IN 2012.

A FAMILY GATHERING AT THE CEMETERY—PROBABLY AN ALL-SAINT'S-DAY.

KIT IN CALCUTTA FOR BASIC TRAINING.

KIT (CENTRE FRONT) WITH THE ADVANCED AIRFORCE GROUP, IN FRONT OF THE P-38, IN THE U.S.

KIT'S PASSPORT AND VISA FROM CALCUTTA TO AMERICA VIA AFRICA

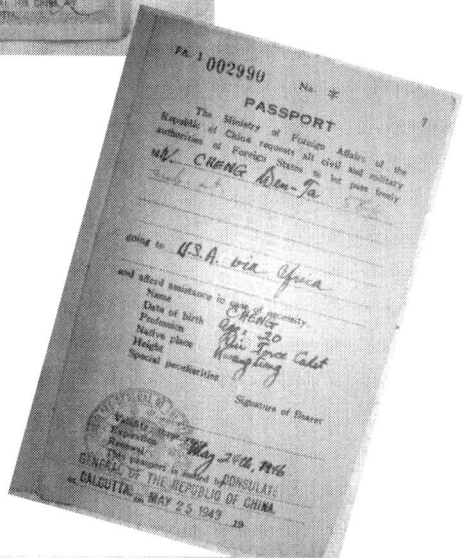

KIT'S LETTERS TO PAUL SENT TO UNCLE S.S. IN CHUNG KING.

KWAN FAMILY GATHERING FOR GRANDUNCLE #12'S BIRTHDAY IN 1949.

THE IMAGE IS TAKEN FROM THE KWAN GENEOLOGY ON LINE.

12TH GREAT UNCLE SUM-MUN'S BIRTHDAY, HONG KONG – 1949.

TEMPLATE OF THE KWAN FAMILY PHOTO SHOWING WHOSE WHO. DR. RICHARD YUNG (8-8-1) DID THE WORK FOR THESE IMAGES.

12th GREAT UNCLE SUM MUN'S BIRTHDAY, HONG KONG - 1949

Back Row (L-R): 1 Joe Lin 7-5-2, 2. Richmond Cheng 7-3-5, 3. Barbara Chew 12-1-1, 4. Faith Ko 9-3-2, 5. –, 6 Siu-Kuan 12-5, 7. Yik-Mun Sun 12-6S,

4th Row: 8. Eddy Tan 12-2S, 9. Iu-Fun Kwan 12-3, 10. Bau Tsu-Zung 2-10S, 11. Steve Siu-Tze 7-15, 12. Bessie Iu-Cheung 12-4, 13. Cecil Leong 12-4S, 14. Weng Hong 13-1, 15. Sek-Kai / Keng-Fun Ko 9-3, 16. Ching-Hsia Chang 6-1S2, 17. –, 18. Rose Yaw-Mun 2-6, 19. Yin-Chin Soong 13-1S2, 20. - , 21 Yaw-Yin 2-4, 22. Yung Kai-Mun 8-1 ?, 23. Martha Yaw-Yuen 2-3, 24. May Sung-Sien Kwan 6-7, 25. Yan-Tse Sun 7-6S, 26. Violet Wai-Fong 7-5, 27. Daisy Wai-Heng 7-3, 28. So-Heng Kwan 9-3, 29. Siu-Yoon 7-16, 30. Yeu-Hing Kwan 2-10, 31. - , 32. Ivy Wai-Chan 7-10, 33. Kwan Sung Sing 6-1, 34. Yeung Wah-Yat.

3rd Row: 35. Wai-Ying Lee 7-8S, 36. Wai-Chong kwan 7-12, 37. Hock-Yuen Kwan 14-4, 38. 13th Gr Aunt Julia Loke 13S, 39. 12th Gr Aunt 12S, 40. 12th Gr Uncle, 41. 7th Gr Aunt 7S2, 2nd Row: 42. Harry Long 7-10S, 43. Phyllis Iu-Chee Kwan 12-2, 44. Betty Iu-Hin 12-8, 45. Ka-Hung Kwan 12-5-1, 46. Edwin Tan 12-2-2, 47. Kin-Loon Kwan 7-6,

Front Row: 48. David Chun-Shi Kwan 2-2-1, 49. Ruth Ho 2-2-1S, 50. Mejorie Mo-Chuen Lee 12-5S, 51. Chu Pin 6-7S, 52. Alan Cheng-Tong Lin 7-5-7, 53. Kenneth Wei-Ming Kwan 6-1, 54. Dennis Leong 12-4-1, 55. Tuck Cheng-Wei Lin 7-5-6, 56. Tony Qi Kwan 14-8, 57. Edwina Tan 12-2-1, 58. Yue-Deen Kwan 9-5, 59. Gloria Mun-Cheok Kwan 7-2-3.

K.T. QUEK 1950

(MY HUSBAND)

AUNTIE EMILY (MOTHER'S DEAR FRIEND FROM K L), CHING, MUNGIE, JIMMY (PAUL'S SON) AND MOTHER. 1962—BEFORE THE MASS EXODUS TO AMERICA.

THE IMPERIAL DISHES—GIVEN TO GRANDUNCLE # 6 WHEN HE
WAS THE EMPRESS DOWAGER'S PERSONAL PHYSICIAN.

THE SOUP TUREENS, THE SMALL POURING POT AND THE ENGLISH
STYLE CUPS AND SAUCERS ARE MENTIONED IN THE STORY.

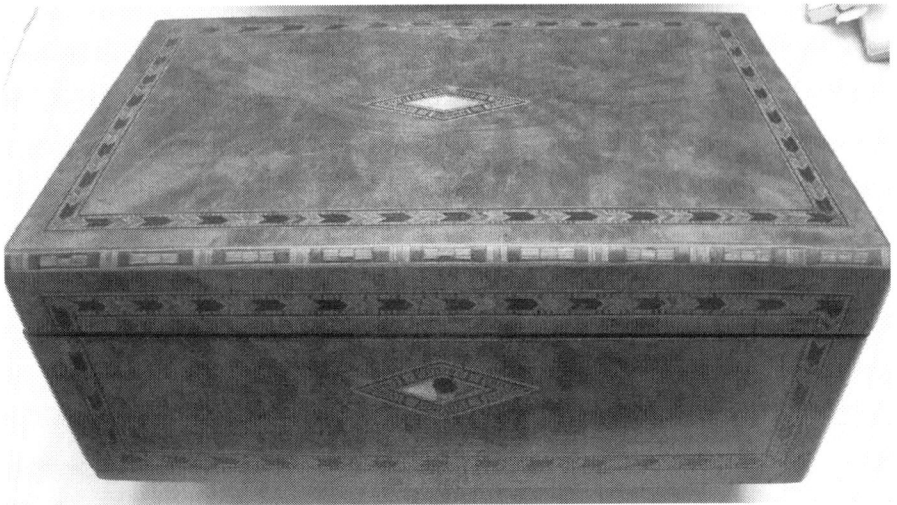

THE ESCRITOIRE (WRITING BOX) FROM GRANDAUNTIE
10'S ROOM. It was given to Great Grandmother Kwan from
her "parents," the Cotswolds, when she earned her nurse's pin.

THE BLUE BOY
THAT HUNG IN
GRANDAUNTIE#
10'S ROOM. IT HAS
A WOODEN BACK
AND HAS A RUSTED
METAL FRAME. It is
a print from the original
oil on canvas by Thomas
Gainsborough—
circa:1770. There was a
German Film called The
Boy In Blue in 1919.
Maybe it made this
painting popular, even in
Hong Kong.

Made in the USA
Lexington, KY
07 July 2014